Non-fiction

Jim Taylor

Published by Letts Educational
The Chiswick Centre
414 Chiswick High Road
London W4 5TF

📞 020 89963333
📠 020 87428390
✉ mail@lettsed.co.uk
🌐 www.letts-education.com

Letts Educational Limited is a division of Granada Learning Limited, part of Granada plc.

First published 2002

ISBN 1840857080

British Library Cataloguing in Publication Data
A catalogue record for this book is available from the British Library.

Developed and packaged by McLean Press Ltd

Commissioned by Helen Clark

Project management by Vicky Butt

Edited by Gavin McLean

Cover design by bigtop, Bicester, UK

Internal design by bigtop, Bicester, UK

Acknowledgements

The publishers would like to thank the following for permission to use copyright material. Every effort has been made to trace copyright holders and to obtain their permission for the use of copyright material. The authors and publishers will gladly receive information enabling them to rectify any error or omission in subsequent editions.

annefine.co.uk pages 33–34, BBC Worldwide pages 65–67, 73, bbc.co.uk pages 76–77, 88–89, carolhurst.com pages 29–31, Computer Shopper pages 61–62, Faber & Faber Ltd pages 45–46, Guardian Media Group page 93, Halifax pages 108–109, Hamish Hamilton Children's Books pages 33–34, IPC Media Ltd page 49, learn.co.uk page 13, Lunn Poly Ltd page 19, McDonald's Restaurants Ltd pages 5–6, Parragon Ltd pages 42, 69–70, Penguin UK pages 37–38, 53–54, 96–97, Sheil Land Associates page 105, Stretford Grammar School pages 112–113, The Ninja Corp. pages 16–17, Trinity Mirror pages 57–59, Western Daily Press pages 22–23.

Illustrations by Linda Combi and Darren Lingard

Production by PDQ

Printed and bound in the UK by Ashford Colour Press

Contents

Key to English Framework Teaching Objectives

R = Reading   SL = Speaking and Listening   W = Writing   Wd = Word   S = Sentence

Recycle, Repackage, Reuse

Aims

● To learn how some leaflets present information in as clear a way as possible.

Starter session

Work with a partner. You should each hold up an object chosen from your school bag. Taking turns, you should try to give as many facts as you can about the object that you have chosen. For example, if a ruler was chosen, you might state:

> 'This ruler is made of plastic.'

The winner is the person who can state the most facts. Choose no more than three objects each.

Introduction

One purpose of a leaflet is to give information. This needs to be done as clearly as possible, so that people reading the leaflet can understand it and what it is trying to say. Read the leaflet opposite from McDonald's, the fast food restaurant group, about its role in protecting the environment.

Our Environment

To ensure a prosperous, healthy and sustainable future for everyone – including our children and our children's children, we need to use resources wisely today…to achieve our 'green goals', Reduce, Reuse and Recycle.

We recognise we have an impact on the environment. We are aware of our responsibilities to reduce this impact and we intend to publish a full environmental report detailing our progress towards meeting our targets. In the meantime here are some of the highlights – projects we're proud of and projects we're sure will help contribute to a cleaner and greener tomorrow.

REDUCE!

McDonald's is a quick service, good value restaurant company offering a range of quality products. We use packaging to ensure our food is fresh, hot, convenient and most importantly – safe. But we are always looking at ways to reduce the amount of packaging we use.

Small changes can deliver big results. For example, last year, we reduced the thickness of our napkins, saving 1500 tonnes of paper, which equates to saving 22,500, average-sized trees.

We have trimmed 22 per cent in weight from each hamburger box in the past few years – from 6 to 4.7g, that means we saved 454 tonnes of plastic.

We are also continually looking to reduce our use of energy. We make use of technology and efficient practices in restaurants, such as:

• Sensors in new restaurants which turn off lighting when not needed

• Computerised energy management systems so equipment is shut down at the correct times

• On going energy surveys and staff education campaigns to encourage turning off lights and unnecessary equipment

REUSE!

We have developed a scheme for restaurants to collect French Fry delivery packaging, which is then reused in the shipping and removal industry.

In the last eight years nearly 5 million boxes were collected for re-sale and the £300,000 raised was donated to Ronald McDonald Children's Charities, which provides accommodation for families with children in hospital for long stay treatment.

BUY RECYCLED!

Wherever possible we use recycled materials in our packaging and are continually reassessing the latest products available. We use:

• 100% recycled paper for
> happy meal boxes
> bags
> drinks trays
> napkins
> kitchen rolls
> toilet tissue

• 75% recycled material in plastic trays in restaurants.

• 72% recycled paper and card food boxes.

• All trayliners are printed on paper produced from elemental chlorine free (ECF) pulp derived from fully sustainable managed forests.

Development

SPEAKING AND LISTENING   **READING**   WRITING

McDonald's are giving you information in this leaflet.

- Information leaflets are produced mainly to present **facts** to those individuals who read them. Facts are usually pieces of information that are true, or can be checked to see if they are true. In pairs, find three facts from the information given. Compare your facts with those of another pair of pupils. As a class, collate the facts identified on the board.

- However, leaflets can also contain **opinions**. Again, in pairs, see if you can identify three opinions given in the leaflet. Compare these also with another pair and collate them on the board. In what way do opinions differ from facts?

- Look at the layout and design of the leaflet. Can you identify some of the ways that the information is presented to make it clear and helpful to the reader? For example, do the short, clear-cut paragraphs help you to understand the leaflet? In what other ways does the design of the leaflet help you understand it?

SPEAKING AND LISTENING   READING   **WRITING**

You are now going to try and write an information leaflet of your own. Choose a topic from the list below:

- The advantages of becoming a vegetarian
- The safest way to get from home to school in the mornings
- Facts about your school for new pupils.

Write a leaflet of your own using similar methods to those you discovered in the McDonald's leaflet. Remember to think carefully about the language you use and the layout (e.g. paragraphs, bullet points and so on).

Review

In this unit you have learnt that information leaflets should try and present the facts of a situation or event clearly so that they can be easily understood. To do so, there are specific ways to structure and present the information they contain.

Children telling tales

Aims

● To learn about differences between speech and writing.

Starter session

Work in groups of three. Two of you should choose a topic from the list below:

● your first day at secondary school
● your first live pop concert or football match
● the day you moved house
● the arrival of a baby sister or brother.

The first person should begin to tell the other two about the topic they have chosen. If they hesitate, it is the turn of the second person to talk about their topic. The person who has not chosen a topic should act as referee, recording the number of hesitations of each of the other two. The winner is the one who hesitates least.

Introduction

There are lots of differences between the way that we speak and the way that we write. One of the ways to see these differences is to write down *exactly* what people say. When you do this you are creating a **transcript**.

You will notice that there are lots of differences between transcripts and the sorts of writing that you do in school. For instance, the symbol (.) in a transcript means that the speaker has paused while speaking.

Development

Read the extracts below:

 (9 year old girl asked to recount a visit to a doctor)

Well one morning I woke up and I got out of bed and my dad was getting ready for work (.) it was four o'clock in the morning and he was getting dressed for work (.) and my mum was making him toast and I think he had honey with it and I told mum I was sick and I couldn't breathe (.) and she asked me what was the matter and I told her (.) and then I told her I wanted my dad (.) so he came out and took me to the hospital (.) brought me in a taxi and my mum came as well (.) and after they got me to the hospital they made sure I was alright and everything (.) and then my dad went to work and my mum went back home to get ready to go to her work

 (5 year old boy asked to recount a past event connected with a circus)

once I've seen a clown (.) I've been to browning's circus (.) the clowns were very funny (.) do you know what they did? (.) one spilled water over his head and do you know what happened? (.) he got up and fell down on the ground again because he had a pie thrown in his face (.) and do you know he threw a pie back at them (.) and then he threw water at the audience and at mummy and me (.) and he tore a hole in his shirt (.) he was wearing a red one (.) and he sat down on a nail and then dragged the nail along (.) and his trousers fell off

I can remember once (.) when I'd just
first come to this school (.) an (.) er (.) went on
beech road with steve miller and jon bate (.) and we'd heard
about these swords (.) a field near eric homes (.) and we went to it (.)
and found that we (.) er (.) we (.) went across this stream and we
couldn't get back (.) and we were saying circle the stream and we tried
(..) we hadn't looked at this part where there was a track leading out (.)
and we tried to cross it to get to the other field where the swords
were (.) so they said (.) and there was this tree going across
on (.) I went on the tree and steve (.) he went on (.) and jon
bate (.) and then jon went home (.) and then steve jolted on
it (.) and we both fell in (.) and we had to swim for the
side (..) but we didn't find these swords

A SPEAKING AND LISTENING   **READING**   **WRITING**

These extracts are examples of transcripts of children talking. They have
been *transcribed* (from an audio cassette) into pieces of writing. The
information in brackets at the beginning of the transcript gives you some
idea of what the children were talking about.

● You have already been given the example of the way that a pause in
  speaking is recorded in a transcript. As you read the transcripts, see how
  many other examples of unusual punctuation you can identify.

- Each person in the group should choose a different transcript and re-write it into the way that you would normally write in school. To help, the first sentence in each transcript has been done for you below.
  - **Extract 1** 'One morning I woke up.'
  - **Extract 2** 'Once I saw a clown.'
  - **Extract 3** 'I can remember when I first came to this school.'
- When you have finished re-writing the transcripts, have a group discussion about the changes that you have made. Think, in particular, about:
  - the ways that you have connected and joined up the phrases
  - how you have paragraphed the writing
  - any changes to verb tenses that you have used.
- Record these changes on a wall chart.

Review

In this unit you have learnt that there are important differences between the way that we write and the way that we speak. For example:

- we tend to pause when we are speaking.
- we sometimes hesitate and repeat ourselves.
- we tend to run phrases and sentences together without the normal punctuation of writing.

Erupting with explanations

Aims

● To learn about how the facts of an event or situation are explained – *why* certain events or situations occur as they do.

Starter session

Work with a partner. From the list below, each of you should choose a different topic. They are all topics you might have come across in other school subjects:

● How the solar system was formed (Science)
● How glaciers occur (Geography)
● How dinosaurs disappeared from the earth (Science)
● Why Hadrian's Wall was built (History)
● How a spaceship gets into outer space (Science).

Take turns to tell your partner as much as you can about the topic that you have chosen. As each of you talks the other should try to record as much of the detail as possible, taking care to try and get the information in the correct order. When each of you has finished you should pass your notes to your partner so that they can check the accuracy of what you have written. Keep these notes as they will be used in a later part of the lesson.

Introduction

In Unit 1 (page 7), you learnt that one purpose of information leaflets is to give us some facts about a particular event or situation. However, another purpose of some information leaflets is to explain in more detail *how* and *why* these facts occur.

Read the explanation sheet opposite on how earthquakes occur and how the force that they generate is measured.

Earthquakes

- The main land areas of earth – the continents like Europe, Asia and North America – 'float' on tectonic plates.
- The points where the edges of these plates meet result in fault lines.
- Earthquakes are caused by movement along a fault line.
- This movement is most common along plate boundaries; especially at compressional plate boundaries.
- As the plates collide and push against each other, the rock snags. This leads to a build up of pressure until the plates jerk apart from each other, resulting in an earthquake.
- The point where earthquakes originate below the ground is called the **focus**.
- The point on the earth's surface directly above the focus is called the epicentre. This is where most damage will occur.
- From the focus, shock waves (also called seismic waves) travel through the ground in different directions.
- The shock waves diminish in power the further they travel from the focus and epicentre.

The diagram below illustrates this:

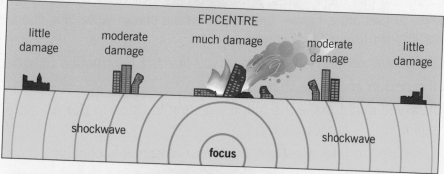

- The magnitude of an earthquake is measured on a seismograph, and given a value from 1 to 10 on the Richter scale. This scale indicates the comparative strengths of earthquakes. Each successive number on the Richter scale indicates an earthquake ten times as strong as the number below it.
- An earthquake measuring 8 on the Richter scale is ten times as powerful as one measuring 7, and a hundred times more powerful than one measuring 6.

Development

SPEAKING AND LISTENING **READING** *WRITING*

In order to explain the facts of an event or situation to us, the information has to be presented in specific ways. For example, in the sixth bullet point, the word 'focus' appears in bold.

- Discuss with your partner why you think the writer has done this.
- Can you identify any other examples of the ways that the information is presented to clearly explain the facts.
- Why do you think the order in which the facts are presented is important?
- Can you identify any other bits of information which are not hard facts, but which might be the opinions or views of the writer.
- What tense and person are used mainly throughout the explanation sheet? Discuss with your partner why tense and person are important.

B **SPEAKING AND LISTENING** *READING* *WRITING*

You are now going to try and produce an explanation of your own.

Look again at the notes which your partner made at the start of the lesson and which you checked.

You should use these notes, and any others which you might want to make, to prepare a formal talk to the whole class, explaining the facts of your chosen topic. Think about:

- the sequence of events and how you link the information together
- the person and tense that you use
- how you might make the talk interesting to listen to (for example, by telling it in a humorous way).

Be prepared to take questions from your classmates once you have finished speaking.

Review

In this unit you have learnt that writing which tries to explain the facts should:

- be clearly sequenced and presented
- highlight and stress important words and phrases
- use visual aids like diagrams, where possible.

Easy does it

Aims

- To learn about instructional writing.

Starter session

A recipe is a familiar piece of writing which tells or **instructs** us how to cook something. With a partner you should each think up an imaginary recipe which you think the rest of the class will find funny, e.g. the recipe for 'headmaster soup'.

Making notes, you should list the main ingredients, the amount of each item to be added, and the way that they are to be mixed in order to arrive at the finished dish.

Once you and your partner have completed your recipe, raise your hands and read it out to the rest of the class.

Introduction

Instructional pieces of writing tell us how to do certain jobs or tasks. A common example would be Do It Yourself (DIY) texts. If you have watched any of your parents trying to put together a piece of furniture bought from the local DIY store, you will remember that they probably had to follow a set of instructions, included in the pack, to assemble the piece.

Instructions need to be written clearly and concisely. No other information is required other than that necessary to complete the task. Most importantly, all of the instructions must appear in the correct order.

Development

A SPEAKING AND LISTENING **READING** WRITING

Look at the instructional leaflet below. It contains the instructions on how to pack away and put up a children's play toy called a Hide A Way Block. As you read the instructions, think about how they are presented and the language which is used. In particular:

- list the imperative or command verbs and verb phrases that are used e.g. 'press down' (in No. 6); how many others can you find?
- say whether the instructions are written in the active or passive voice
- identify any other features of the leaflet which help the reader to understand the instructions.

How to pack away your Hide A Way Block safely.

IMPORTANT. The putting up and taking down of the Hide A Way Block should <u>always</u> be done by a responsible adult.

1. To collapse the Hide A Way Block, push any corner in towards an opposite corner.
2. Then fold flat.
3. Keeping hold of the edges, turn the block upside down.
4. Pressing down (with your thumbs on top of the rim and your fingers underneath it), bow the block outwards.
5. When it is almost bowed double, curl the rim held in your right hand back in under the rim held in your left hand. Then curl the left-hand side over.
6. Press down to fold the block flat and (without letting go!) slide it back into its bag.

It's a simple as that!

The putting up of your Hide A Way Block is just as easy.

1. Carefully remove from its bag.
2. Open up the top ring.
3. The block should then just pop open.
4. Open up the two halves of the block as you would a book.
5. Pull out the other side of the block and it should just pop open and it will be ready to play in.

A SPEAKING AND LISTENING   **READING**   WRITING

You are now going to try and write a piece of instructional writing of your own. Imagine that you have just been given the job of running a new school tuck shop which is to be opened during school morning and afternoon breaks and at lunchtime.

- Write a set of instructions for the other pupils who will be buying items from the tuck shop. Remember the purpose of the instructions is to ensure that the tuck shop runs smoothly and efficiently. Use ICT to present the instructions clearly. To help you, a possible way to start is suggested below.

Opening of St. Trinian's Tuck Shop
1. The new tuck shop will open inside the main hall.
2. The opening times will be as follows:

Review

In this unit you have learnt that instructional writing tends to:
- contain precise information only on the task in hand
- contain information which is clearly sequenced and place in the correct order
- contain lots of imperative verbs
- be written in the active voice.

Persuaded by 'The Big Apple'

Aims

- To learn about and demonstrate an understanding of **persuasive** writing.

Starter session

Two members of the class should volunteer to write the names of two world famous cities (other than New York) on the blackboard. As a class, you should brainstorm any information you are able to come up with on each of the chosen cities, calling out as you go along. The information should be recorded on the board, in the form of a spider diagram.

Introduction

Persuasive writing generally has a specific purpose. For example, much persuasive writing is found in adverts which are aimed at getting us to buy something. You will find the following features in this type of writing:

- In order to get its message across, key points tend to be repeated.
- There is a lot of information given which is not crucial to the main points being made.
- Words and pictures are combined so that we get as full a view as possible of what is on offer.

Development

A SPEAKING AND LISTENING   READING   WRITING

Look at the holiday brochure extract for New York City which appears opposite.

Big, brash, vibrant and dynamic – its energy will sweep you off your feet. Love it or hate it you certainly won't forget it.

SIGHTSEEING

So much to see and do in the city that never stops. For breathtaking views of the city climb the Empire State Building. Saunter the streets of Greenwich Village and Soho which are bustling at night and daytime. Take the Staten Island Ferry trip (for free) and get great views of the Statue of Liberty and Manhattan Skyline. Take a walk up Fifth Avenue, 42nd Street and Madison Avenue and discover the delights on offer. If you are looking for hustle, bustle and a great atmosphere, walk around Times Square at any hour of the day and you will be caught up in the overwhelming ambience – truly an experience to be had.

Uptown/Downtown City Loop   £30pp
See the sights of New York city in both Uptown and Downtown Manhattan. A guide will tell you about the development of the unique city. From Greenwich Village to Brooklyn Bridge and from Central Park to Harlem Market. The bonus of this tour – the price includes unlimited hop-on/hop-off use of the Double Decker for 24 hours. The Downtown Loop is 2 hours and the Uptown loop is 3 hours.

The Big Apple Helicopter Tour   from £70pp
(Sun-Sat) 10–12 mins
Take a ride by air through the world's most famous skyline. The Statue of Liberty, the Empire State Building and the Chrysler Building will seem so close you can almost touch them.

Harlem on Sunday*   £54pp
Attend an authentic church service in Harlem where you will hear soul-stirring gospel music. Complete your morning with some of the best Soul Food and Gospel music at a top restaurant.

BY NIGHT

Nights on Broadway*   from £78pp
Enjoy a top Broadway show at the end of a day of shopping. A must for all visitors to Manhattan. Tickets are for mid-range seats.

Available by request only. Please call our Reservations Team for details.

- What is this extract trying to do? (What is its purpose?)
- Would you be persuaded to visit New York after you have read this extract? Why? You should give reasons for your answers.
- What other features of the writing are important? For example, think about what the pictures add to the writing. Would the extract be persuasive if it had to rely on the writing alone?
- How many other features of the writing can you identify which help to get its message across? Think about the language used, the paragraphs, the layout of the information, and so on.
- Can you identify any negative points being made about New York. Why do you think this is the case?
- In the extract, the costs of various sight-seeing tours and attractions are given in UK pounds sterling and not in US dollars. Why do you think this is the case?

B SPEAKING AND LISTENING | READING | *WRITING*

You are now going to try and produce your own piece of persuasive writing. Think about your own home town or city.
- Produce a holiday brochure entry, intended to persuade would-be holiday-makers to visit your home town or city, and to spend some time there.
- You should emphasise the key points.
- You should also try to include as much visual information as you can.
- Add as much information as you can on local places of interest.
- If you are stuck for information, you might like to search for information about your town or city on the Internet.

Review

In this unit you have learnt that a certain type of persuasive writing is designed to advertising places or things. In order to persuade us to part with our money:
- the language used has to be clear and very positive in tone –
- the information should be clearly set out using:
  – short paragraphs, lots of bold type, different print fonts (gloss)
- key points are emphasised and repeated
- pictures are used to 'get the message across'.

A hair-raising incident!

Aims

- To learn about discursive writing. This type of writing tends to present an opinion on a topic or issue, on which there is a lot of debate.

Starter session

Mobile phones are now owned and used by most of the population, particularly young people. Many schools discourage students from using their phones during school hours and have a policy on the subject.

Think about your own views on the subject. Those members of the class who are in favour of using phones during school hours should stand up and give their reasons, followed by those who are against. The positive and negative points on the debate should be recorded in two columns on the board.

At the end, a vote should be taken to see whether as a whole, the class is either in favour or against using phones in school hours.

Introduction

Discursive writing tends to take sides – it comes down either in favour or against an argument about a person, issue or event. But before it takes sides, a good piece of discursive writing will explore both sides of the argument, stressing the strengths and weaknesses of each side. In finally coming to a point of view, the writer will usually give reasons why s/he has arrived at this particular conclusion.

Development

Read the newspaper article below, entitled 'Banned pupil fights for the right to tint his hair'. It is about a boy pupil who has been excluded from school for dyeing his hair blond.

- While you are reading, try to identify and write down the opposing viewpoints being expressed, either in favour of the boy's case, or against it.
- What is your view generally of school pupils being allowed to dye their hair? Give reasons for your answer.

Western Daily Press 3 April 2000

Banned pupil fights for right to tint his hair

By Beverley Hawes

A SCHOOL that sent a boy home last week for having a stud in his ear is now punishing another pupil for dyeing his hair blond.

Philip Wood has been told his bleached locks break rules on the appearance of pupils at St Benedict's Catholic High School, Cheltenham, and he has been put on indefinite afternoon detention.

He has also been removed from classroom lessons to study alone after he had the top of his ear pierced.

Last week another pupil, Richard Gore, aged 13, of Millbrook Gardens, Cheltenham, was sent home after he refused to remove a stud from his left ear.

His mother Christine, aged 35, accused the school of discrimination because girls at the school are allowed to wear studs.

Now Philip's mother Caroline, aged 39, of Kingsmead Avenue, Cheltenham is also supporting her son's bleached look.

She said: 'I'm angry – this is not fair. The school's policy is wrong. Philip had his hair highlighted with my permission and I think it suits him.

'I'd understand it if Philip looked scruffy but he doesn't. He takes pride in his appearance.

'Philip has missed school over this. Why should his education suffer just because of an earring or hair colour? It's not as if he dyed it blue or purple.

'The school is much harder on boys than girls, which is unfair.'

And Philip said: 'The school's policy is not fair. This is an important year for me and I can't afford to miss anything.'

The school's headteacher, John Murray, said he could not discuss individual cases but added: 'Our uniform policy says pupils' hair colour and haircuts should not be extreme.

'Hair colour should be natural and discreet. Natural looking highlights are allowed. Extremes are strictly banned.

'We have this policy because schools are about learning, not about fashion.'

B SPEAKING AND LISTENING   READING   **WRITING**

You are now going to try and produce your own piece of discursive writing. Look again at the notes for and against using mobile phones in school which were recorded on the board at the beginning of the lesson.

● Write an essay, in no more than 250 words, setting out the case for and against using mobile phones in school. You should finish with a paragraph or two giving your own views on the matter, and the reasons why you feel the way you do.

Review

In this unit you have learnt the rules involved in discursive or opinionated writing. This form of non-fiction writing usually involves the clear discussion of an issue or event where there are at least two opposing viewpoints, with a case being made in favour of one of these.

Things are hotting up!

Aims

- To learn about the main features of writing a scientific report.

Starter session

The class should be split into two teams.

In your teams you should think about the sorts of things that you are currently doing as part of your school Science lessons. How do Science lessons differ from, say, English lessons? Think about:

- the differences in the subject matter of each
- the language used in discussion and writing about each
- how any conclusions or findings are recorded in each.

Someone from each team should stand up and make a point about these differences. That person should then nominate someone from the other team to make the next point. If that person fails to make a point the team nominating gets a point. The winning team is the one with the most points. The teacher will act as the referee.

Introduction

Scientific reports try to present facts, following some sort of scientific explanation. In general, the main stages of any scientific investigation involve:

- stating what it is that you wish to prove (e.g. in the case opposite, that the Earth is getting warmer). This is known as the **hypothesis**.
- conducting some scientific research or experiment which will either prove or fail to support the hypothesis
- producing some conclusions or findings in the form of a written scientific report.

Development

A SPEAKING AND LISTENING   **READING**   WRITING

Read the scientific report below, on global warming, the greenhouse effect and climate change. This report was specifically written with a teenage audience in mind. Are there specific uses of language that identify this report as written for this audience? As you read, try to think about the information which is presented in this scientific report.

- Does it contain facts or opinions, e.g. 'greenhouse gases make the earth warmer by trapping energy in the atmosphere'?
- How can you judge whether the views expressed are true or false?
- How do you think the writer was able to come up with the information which s/he presents?
- Could this information be argued against or challenged in any way?

Back   Forward   Stop   Refresh   Home   AutoFill   Print   Mail

Global Warming: What It Is…

Earth has warmed by about 1˚F over the past 100 years. But why? And how? Well, scientists are not exactly sure. The Earth could be getting warmer on its own, but many of the world's leading climate scientists think that things people do are helping to make the Earth warmer.

Greenhouse Effect and Global Warming

The Greenhouse Effect: Scientists are sure about the greenhouse effect. They know that greenhouse gases make the Earth warmer by trapping energy in the atmosphere.

Global Warming: Global warming refers to an average increase in the Earth's average temperature, which in turn causes changes in climate. A warmer Earth may lead to changes in rainfall patterns, a rise in sea level, and a wide range of impacts on plants, wildlife, and humans. When scientists talk about the issue of climate change, their concern is about global warming caused by human activities.

Greenhouse Effect...

The greenhouse effect is the rise in temperature that the Earth experiences because certain gases in the atmosphere (water vapour, carbon dioxide, nitrous oxide, and methane, for example) trap energy from the sun. Without these gases, heat would escape back into space and Earth's average temperature would be about 60°F colder. Because of how they warm our world, these gases are referred to as greenhouse gases.

Have you ever seen a greenhouse? Most greenhouses look like a small glass house. Greenhouses are used to grow plants, especially in the winter. Greenhouses work by trapping heat from the sun. The glass panels of the greenhouse let in light but keep heat from escaping. This causes the greenhouse to heat up, much like the inside of a car parked in sunlight, and keeps the plants warm enough to live in the winter.

The Earth's atmosphere is all around us. It is the air that we breathe. Greenhouse gases in the atmosphere behave much like the glass panes in a greenhouse. Sunlight enters the Earth's atmosphere, passing through the blanket of greenhouse gases. As it reaches the Earth's surface, land, water, and biosphere absorb the sunlight's energy. Once absorbed, this energy is sent back into the atmosphere. Some of the energy passes back into space, but much of it remains trapped in the atmosphere by the greenhouse gases, causing our world to heat up.

The greenhouse effect is important. Without the greenhouse effect, the Earth would not be warm enough for humans to live. But if the greenhouse effect becomes stronger, it could make the Earth warmer than usual. Even a little extra warming may cause problems for humans, plants, and animals.

You are now going to try and produce your own scientific report.

It is generally accepted that there is a direct link between smoking tobacco and the causes of lung cancer. This provides us with an initial hypothesis, i.e. that smoking tobacco causes lung cancer.

Use the library and/or ICT and the Internet to:

- gather as much information as you can on the links between tobacco and lung cancer
- present your findings in the form of a scientific report.

Use the following headings to structure your report:

- Hypothesis
- Research/Investigation
- Findings/Conclusions

Your report should contain enough research information to support your conclusions.

Think carefully about the way that you present your report. Remember that if you use evidence which is not your own to support your conclusions, you must acknowledge the sources, by writing down where this information came from.

Review

In this unit you have learnt the main points to be followed when writing a scientific report. You have also learnt something about the methods to be followed when conducting a piece of scientific research.

The complete Harry Potter experience

Aims

- To learn about the main features of writing and reading book reviews.

Starter session

Who hasn't heard of Harry Potter? The Harry Potter books are a major publishing success worldwide and, of course, a major movie has now been made of the first book in the series, *Harry Potter and the Philosopher's Stone*.

Working with a partner, each of you should write down six pieces of information which you know about the Harry Potter stories. Exchange these with your partner and get her/him to arrange them into order of importance, starting with the most important. Talk through with your partner why you chose this particular order.

Introduction

Book reviews are written for a variety of purposes. For example, they may be produced by the publishers of a book to increase its sales – however, such reviews tend to be uncritical and give a one-sided, glowing view of the book.

On the other hand, many newspapers and magazines have book review sections, where the latest books are regularly reviewed. Increasingly, book reviews are also to be found on the Internet.

Development

SPEAKING AND LISTENING **READING** WRITING

Read the book review below on the first three Harry Potter books. As you read, try to think about:

● why book reviews are written

● where they would generally appear

● what sort of people would write them

● what sort of people would read them.

If you haven't already read any of these Harry Potter books would reading this review make you want either to go out and buy the books, or borrow them from the library? Give reasons for your answers.

Following the title *Harry Potter and the Chamber of Secrets*, some reference information appears in brackets '(Arthur A. Levine/ Scholastic, 1999 ISBN 0439064864. Hardcover, Cassette)'. What does this information refer to and why do you think it has been included as part of the review?

What do you think are the main difficulties involved in writing a book review? For example:

● Is the length of the book an important factor?

● Should the review contain both the positive and the negative aspects of the book?

REVIEW

You have to have been living in a box not to know about the literary phenomenon of Harry Potter. Not since Roald Dahl's *Charlie and the Chocolate Factory* have I seen such widespread acceptance of a single title by thousands of kids and grown-ups. The fact that the books are well written, exciting works of fantasy makes them a gold mine for anyone interested in promoting reading. That adults are reading and enjoying them on their own without the help or excuse of a child interpreter makes the phenomenon even more remarkable. Are they the best fantasies ever written? Probably not, but they are far above run of the mill.

In Harry Potter we get every little guy's fantasy of a physically weak but smart hero vanquishing villains of far greater strength and power. It's the Br'er Rabbit syndrome: the small ones use wit and humour to get the best of the big, powerful ones.

Start by reading the first Harry Potter book, *Harry Potter and the Philosopher's Stone*.

Harry Potter's life among the 'Muggles' (ordinary humans) and particularly among his tasteless and cruel relatives will remind you of that of poor James with his rotten aunts in Dahl's *James and the Giant Peach*. This time it's an aunt, uncle and cousin who are the ghastly ones. Harry's life is terrible indeed until a mysterious letter from Hagrid, a friendly giant, informs him that he has been accepted at Hogwarts School of Witchcraft and Wizardry. (It turns out that Harry has been receiving other related mail but it has been intercepted by his evil relatives.)

At Hogwarts, Harry Potter is surrounded by friends and like-minded individuals. That's where the real adventure begins. It turns out that Harry's parents were killed by an evil wizard – a creature so evil that others are afraid to speak his name but we'll utter it here: Voldemort. It was at the time of their deaths that Harry got the lightning-shaped scar on his forehead that would later identify him.

Now Harry must find out a good many things: Who is the Man with Two Faces? What's hidden on the third floor of Hogworts Castle? He must also find out what he himself is capable of doing and being. Even wonderful schools such as Hogwarts have holidays, however, and in *Harry Potter and the Chamber of Secrets* (Arthur A. Levine/Scholastic, 1999 ISBN 0439064864. Hardcover, Cassette), Harry Potter has spent a terrible summer with the Dursleys. They even stop him from boarding the train to take him back to Hogwarts at the end of the summer. It's one hazard after another until Harry gets to the safety of the school, but how safe is it?

Evil voices whisper to Harry through the walls. Another student seems to have it in for him. Then mysterious words appear on the wall, 'The Chamber of Secrets Has Been Opened. Enemies of the Heir, Beware'. Harry and his wizard friends Hermione and Ron succeed in cracking the mystery but not without a large dose of humour and suspense.

In *Harry Potter and the Prisoner of Azkaban*, Harry has managed to infuriate the Dursleys by causing a particularly obnoxious visitor, Aunt Marge, to inflate like a balloon and drift upward to the ceiling. Since using wizardry when among Muggles is strictly forbidden, Harry has angered the officials at Hogwarts – at least he thinks he has. With only his pet owl, Hedwig, Harry leaves the Dursleys and is whisked off in a purple bus to an inn called 'The Leaky Cauldron'. There he spends the rest of the summer. Again, however, the real adventure begins when school starts and Harry learns that Sirius Black, an escaped prisoner, is after him.

There you have a not very complete summary of the action so far. *Harry Potter and the Prisoner of Azkaban* is the third volume in the series, but it's not the end. The author, JK Rowling, has many more in store for lovers of fantasy, magic and suspense.

A SPEAKING AND LISTENING   READING   **WRITING**

You are now going to try and write your own book review.

- Think about a book that you have been reading lately. This could either be a book which you have read as part of your English lessons, or at home, in your spare time.

- In no more than 250 words, write a review of this book stressing:
  - what the story is about
  - who the main characters are
  - why you liked or disliked the book, giving reasons for your answers.

Review

In this unit you have learnt the main aspects involved in writing a book review. You have also learnt something about why they are written and whom they are intended for. In order to get a clear picture of what a book is about, you need to read it! However, a book review might give you some quick information on a book which you intend to read either for study or pleasure.

An extremely fine author

Aims

- To compare, contrast and evaluate information text from different sources.

Starter session

We get our information on events and people – real or fictional – from a number of different sources. Go around the class, shouting out different sources of information. You can think about lots of different types of information, including:

- information you take in generally as part of your everyday life
- information you need for your school work
- information you receive in the form of entertainment.

To start you off, here are two quite different sources:

1 a morning newspaper
2 school assembly.......

Try to see if you can get around the whole class before you run out of ideas.

Introduction

We are bombarded with information most of the hours that we are awake. For example:

- when we wake in the morning we might listen to the radio or watch breakfast TV
- in school our teachers give us more information as part of our education
- when we come home in the evening we might watch some more TV or read a newspaper
- we might play a computer game or surf the Internet
- we might go to a movie.

The point is that whether we are being educated or entertained we are constantly receiving information from a variety of sources. Some of this information will inevitably be about the same topic but received from different sources, e.g. the evening newspaper might cover the same topic which you first saw on breakfast TV, but from a more up-to-date viewpoint.

Development

A SPEAKING AND LISTENING **READING** WRITING

Anne Fine is one of the leading writers of children's fiction. Printed below are four extracts written about her.

- Who do you think is the intended audience for each extract?
- What differences are there between the four extracts? For example, they differ in length, but what other differences can you identify?
- Which do you find the most helpful and why?
- Why do you think that it is important to know about the personal details and background of an author or any other well-known person?

TEXT **1**

Anne Fine is a distinguished writer for children of all ages, with over forty books to her credit. As well as being chosen as Children's Laureate in 2001, she is twice winner of the Carnegie Medal, Britain's most coveted children's literature award, and has also won the Guardian Children's Literature Award, the Whitbread Children's Novel Award twice, and a Smarties Prize. She won the Publishing News Children's Author of the Year Award in 1990 and again in 1993.

Her books for older children include the award winning *The Tulip Touch* and *Goggle-Eyes*, which was adapted for television by the BBC. Twentieth Century Fox filmed her novel *Madame Doubtfire* as *Mrs Doubtfire*, starring Robin Williams. Her books for younger children include *Bill's New Frock* and *How to Write Really Badly*. Her work has been translated into twenty-five languages.

Anne Fine has also written for adults. Her novels *The Killjoy, Taking the Devil's Advice, In Cold Domain, Telling Liddy* and, most recently, *All Bones and Lies*, have been published to considerable critical acclaim.

Anne Fine has two grown up daughters, and lives in County Durham.

Anne Fine was born in Leicester and has lived in both Canada and in the United States. She is married with two daughters and her permanent home is now Edinburgh. Her earlier books for children include *The Summer House Loon*, *The Granny Project*, *A Pack of Lias and Madame Doubtfire*, which was shortlisted for The Observer Teenage Fiction Prize and was runner-up for the Guardian Children's Fiction Award.

London, May 16 2001: Anne Fine was named as the second Children's Laureate. The announcement was made by Poet Laureate, Andrew Motion, during a ceremony at Waterstone's Bookshop in Piccadilly, London.

The role of Children's Laureate, which has a bursary of £10,000, is awarded once every two years to an eminent writer or illustrator of children's books, to celebrate outstanding achievement in their field. The appointment of a Children's Laureate acknowledges the importance of exceptional children's authors in creating the readers of tomorrow.

The Laureateship was the original idea of the award–winning children's novelist Michael Morpurgo. Former Poet Laureate, Ted Hughes, was the patron and close supporter of the award until his death in October 1998.

Anne Fine – publications/awards
Children's Laureate

Bad Dreams – shortlisted for WH Smith Book Awards 2001

Charm School – shortlisted for Sheffield Children's Book Award 2000

1999 – shortlisted for the First Children's Laureate Award

1998 – UK nominee for the Hans Christian Andersen Author Award

The Tulip Touch – winner of the Whitbread Children's Book Award, 1996; highly commended, Carnegie Medal, 1997; shortlisted fo the Sheffield Children's Book Award, 1997; runner up for the Lancs Library Children's Book of the Year; Wirral Paperback of the Year, 1998

You are now going to try and present a formal talk to the rest of the class, stressing the main points of your subject matter. This talk should not be any longer than five minutes.

In discussion with a partner:

● Choose a well-known person who you admire and who interests you.

● From what you already know about your subject and/or by using the library and/or the Internet, gather as much information as you can on your chosen individual.

● You may choose any individual that you like, e.g. a pop star, a sports personality, someone famous from history and so on.

● Think carefully about editing down the information you have gathered so that it can fit into a five-minute talk. Why did you decide to leave out some pieces of information and include others?

If possible, you should take it in turns, practising to deliver your talk to your partner, before addressing the whole class. When you have presented your talk to the class, review your performance with your partner:

● Was your talk clearly presented?

● Did you keep to time?

● Did you have too much, or too little information?

● What lessons have you learnt for future presentations?

Review

In this unit you have learnt that information appears in a variety of forms and lengths. You have also learnt that how the information is written and presented depends on its intended audience.

A stranger in a strange land

Aims

● To learn about the conventions of biographical and autobiographical writing.

Starter session

Work with a partner. Think about your family background:

● where your parents come from
● where you were born
● how many brothers and sisters you have
● your grandparents, aunts, uncles, cousins and so on.

Each of you should choose four relatives each. On a separate piece of paper for each relative, list four pieces of information – e.g. how old they are, how tall they are, the colour of their hair and what sort of person they are (happy, sad, serious, funny) and so on. Cut up the pieces of paper so that the names of the relatives are on one pile and the information about them is on another pile. Mix each of these piles up and take turns to produce new identities for the eight relatives chosen.

What do you think about these 'new identities'? Are they believable? Are they funny? Do they make any sense at all?

Introduction

An **autobiography** is an account of aspects of a person's life, written by that person her/himself. A **biography** is an account of aspects of a person's life, written by another person. In the extract below, Laurie Lee's account of his arrival in Spain is clearly written by himself. It is therefore, autobiographical. Autobiographical writing is always written in the first person, using the family of pronouns including *I*, *me*, *we*, *our*, *mine* and so on. By contrast, biographical writing uses the third person voice including pronouns like *he*, *she*, *they*, *his*, *hers*, *theirs* and so on.

Development

A SPEAKING AND LISTENING | **READING** | WRITING

Read the extract below. As you read, think about:

- the language the author uses and how he tries to hold your interest. For example, look at the phrases '…the unconscious rocking of sea…' and '…the rattling anchor going over the side…'. How many other examples of this sort of **imaginative** or **figurative** language can you identify from the extract?

- Do you have any way of knowing if these events actually happened to the author.

- Do you find them believable? Give reasons for your answer.

Into Spain

It was early and still almost dark when our ship reached the harbour, and when out of the unconscious rocking of sea and sleep I was simultaneously woken and hooked to the coast of Spain by the rattling anchor going over the side.

[continued over page]

Lying safe in the old ship's blowsy care, I didn't want to move at first. I'd enjoyed the two slow days coming down the English Channel and across the Bay of Biscay, smelling the soft Gulf winds blowing in from the Atlantic and feeling the deep easy roll of the ship. But this was Vigo, the name on my ticket, and as far as its protection would take me. So I lay for a while in the anchored silence and listened to the first faint sounds of Spain – a howling dog, the gasping spasms of a donkey, the thin sharp cry of a cockerel. Then I packed and went up on to the shining deck, and the Spanish sun rose too, and for the first time in my life I saw, looped round the bay, the shape of a foreign city.

I'd known nothing till then but the smoother surfaces of England, and Vigo struck me like an apparition. It seemed to rise from the sea like some rust-corroded wreck, as old and bleached as the rocks around it. There was no smoke or movement among the houses. Everything looked barnacled, rotting, and deathly quiet, as though awaiting the return of the Flood. I landed in a town submerged by wet green sunlight and smelling of the waste of the sea. People lay sleeping in doorways, or sprawled on the ground, like bodies washed up by the tide.

But I was in Spain, and the new life beginning. I had a few shillings in my pocket and no return ticket; I had a knapsack, blanket, spare shirt, and a fiddle, and enough words to ask for a glass of water. So the chill of dawn left me and I began to feel better. The drowned men rose from the pavements and stretched their arms, lit cigarettes, and shook the night from their clothes. Bootblacks appeared, banging their brushes together, and strange vivid girls went down the streets, with hair like coils of dripping tar and large mouths, red and savage.

Still a little off balance I looked about me, saw obscure dark eyes and incomprehensible faces, crumbling walls scribbled with mysterious graffiti, an armed policeman sitting on the Town Hall steps, and a photograph of Marx in the barber's window. Nothing I knew was here, and perhaps there was a moment of panic – anyway I suddenly felt the urge to get moving. So I cut the last cord and changed my shillings for pesetas, bought some bread and fruit, left the seaport behind me and headed straight for the open country.

Vocabulary

Bootblacks – shoe polishers

Marx – Karl Marx (1818–83) German thinker and hero of Spanish Republicans

Development

B SPEAKING AND LISTENING   READING   **WRITING**

You are now going to try and produce your own piece of autobiographical writing.

Think back to an important event which has happened in your own life and write an autobiographical account of it in no more than 250 words. For example, it might be about something that has happened in your family or with your friends:

● the birth of a baby brother or sister

● a marriage

● a family holiday

● a strange journey

● an outing to the movies, a disco, a football match.

Think carefully about the language which you need to use to make this account clearly autobiographical and interesting to someone other than yourself.

Review

In this unit you have learnt some of the main features of autobiographical and biographical writing, particularly paying attention to the language which you need to use to keep the interest of the reader.

'To boldly go...'

Aims

● To learn more about the language of science investigation.

Starter session

The class should be split into two teams.

In your teams, think about what you know about science and scientific discovery. Members of each team should raise their hands when they have thought of a scientific discovery, and should be prepared to speak for a couple of sentences, briefly explaining the discovery. Three examples are given below to help get you started.

Discovery	Explanation
Atomic particles	All matter, whether living or dead is made up of atoms. They are the basic building blocks of the universe.
The importance of water	Water is vital to the survival of life on Earth. All plants and animals need water to survive.
Gravity	All objects are influenced by gravity. It is the invisible force that pulls everything downwards to the ground.

One point will be awarded for the naming of the discovery and an additional point for the brief explanation. Each team should take it in turn to answer. Your teacher will act as the referee.

At the end of the game, add up the points to decide the winning team. You could also choose one member's discovery and explanation as the overall winner.

Introduction

Most ideas or discoveries which might seem simple and straightforward, are, in reality, very complex. Take, for example, the following statements:

- 'Birds can fly'
- 'Motor cars travel along the road'
- 'The TV is powered by electricity'.

These are all obvious statements of fact that no one would dispute. The difficulty comes in trying to explain them:

- How is it that birds can fly?
- How do motor cars travel along the road?
- What is electricity and how does it power TV?

It is necessary, therefore, to be able to explain complex ideas and scientific principles clearly.

Development

 A SPEAKING AND LISTENING   **READING**   WRITING

Read the extract below entitled 'Exploring Space'. As you read:

- Think about what you are reading and how it differs from one of the books that you are reading as part of your English lessons. List the main differences.
  - What differences are there in the way that the paragraphs are set out?
  - Most of the books that you read for English will not have pictures in them. Do these pictures and illustrations add anything to the writing as a whole?
- The language used by the writer is very direct and matter of fact. Look at the description of 'Moon landings':

> 'The Apollo missions planned to land people on the moon. First to set foot on the lunar surface was Neil Armstrong of Apollo 11, on 20 July 1969. Five further...'

  - Why do you think the writer chose this style?
  - Does it make it easier or more difficult to understand what is being explained?

Exploring space

THE SPACE AGE BEGAN on 4 October 1957, with the launch of the satellite *Sputnik 1* by the former Soviet Union. This was a simple metal ball about 58 centimetres across and 84 kilograms in weight, containing a radio transmitter and a thermometer. The world was stunned. Today there is about one space mission each week, as a launch vehicle blasts free of our planet's gravity and delivers its payload into Earth's orbit – or beyond.

Launch vehicles

The launcher is the most powerful type of engine available, the rocket engine. It must escape the pull of Earth's gravity, which means achieving orbital velocity – a speed of 27,350 kilometres per hour at a height of some 160 kilometres. Following this path, a spacecraft's tendency to go in a straight line, according to the third law of motion, is balanced by the tendency of Earth's gravity to pull it downwards. So the craft follows a curved path, falling endlessly to the surface as the surface curves endlessly away.

Moon landings

The Apollo missions planned to land people on the Moon. First to set foot on the lunar surface was Neil Armstrong of Apollo 11, on 20 July 1969. Five further missions followed, carrying out experiments and taking measurements and bringing back samples of Moon rocks for analysis. The last mission was Apollo 17, in December 1972. The next space missions taking people to another world may be to Mars, around 2020. The journey would take about nine months each way.

You are now going to try and produce a piece of writing of your own which will explain a complex idea or process.

Choose a subject which you are studying in Year 8 and an area within that subject that you have recently covered in class, for example:

● Science – how Friction works

● Maths – what Probability is

● Design and Technology – how a clock works

● Geography – how water pollution occurs

● History – how the Great Fire of London started and spread.

These are only suggestions, so if you have better ideas, use them.

Refer again to the extract on 'Exploring Space' before you begin and remind yourself of the following in order to be as clear as possible:

● the language and style used

● paragraphing and layout

● pictures and diagrams.

Your explanation should be no more than 200 words long. If you do not have access to ICT – which might allow you to include some pictures – you should allow room in your explanation for at least one picture or diagram, which you can describe or sketch in.

Review

In this unit you have looked in detail at how complex ideas and scientific principles are explained. In order to make the writing clear, care and attention must be given to:

● the language used and the style adopted

● the use of short sentences and clear paragraphing

● layout and presentation.

Women and children first!

Aims

- To learn about writing which consists mainly of a personal account by the writer.

Starter session

Look at the following four headings and nominate someone to write them on the board:

- Something that made me happy
- Something that made me sad
- Something that made me frightened
- Something that made me angry.

Think back to an experience that you have had which might fit into one of these headings. Once you have thought it through for a couple of minutes, raise your hand and recount it to the rest of the class. Think about the language you use so that you can keep the attention of your audience. Your teacher will record the number of accounts under each heading. This will give some indication as to whether, as a class, you are happy, sad, frightened or angry!

Introduction

Much of the writing that appears under the heading of non-fiction is written from personal experience. This is obviously the case with autobiographical writing. There is a form of autobiographical writing, however, which records news and important current events, from the perspective of an individual account. This type of writing is known as **reportage**. However, the appeal of reportage is that although it is a personal record, in many cases, because of the historical importance of the subject matter, the writing appeals to a wider audience.

Development

Read the piece of reportage below which is an eyewitness account of the sinking of the luxury liner *The Titanic* in 1912. As you read, think about and make notes on:

- why this is such an interesting account
- the voice or person which the writer uses and why this is important
- how the tension builds as the account progresses
- whether things actually happened as Mrs DH Bishop describes them.

The *Titanic*: From a Lifeboat, 15 April 1912

We did not begin to understand the situation till we were perhaps a mile or more away from the Titanic. Then we could see the rows of lights along the decks begin to slant gradually upwards from the bow. Very slowly the lines of light began to point downward at a greater and greater angle. The sinking was so slow that you could not perceive the lights of the deck changing their position. The slant seemed to be greater about every quarter of an hour. That was the only difference.

In a couple of hours, though, she began to go down more rapidly. Then the fearful sight began. The people in the ship were just beginning to realize how great their danger was. When the forward part of the ship dropped suddenly at a faster rate, so that the upward slope became marked, there was a sudden rush of passengers on all the decks towards the stern. It was like a wave. We could see the great black mass of people in the steerage sweeping to the rear part of the boat and breaking through in to the upper decks. At the distance of about a mile we could distinguish everything through the night, which was perfectly clear. We could make out the increasing excitement on board the boat as the people, rushing to and fro, caused the deck lights to disappear and reappear as they passed in front of them.

This panic went on, it seemed, for an hour. Then suddenly the ship seemed to shoot up out of the water and stand there perpendicularly. It seemed to us that it stood upright in the water for four full minutes.

Then it began to slide gently downwards. Its speed increased as it went down head first, so that the stern shot down with a rush.

The lights continued to burn till it sank. We could see the people packed densely in the stern till it was gone...

[continued over page]

As the ship sank we could hear the screaming a mile away. Gradually it became fainter and fainter and died away. Some of the lifeboats that had room for more might have gone to their rescue, but it would have meant that those who were in the water would have swarmed aboard and sunk her.

You are now going to try and produce your own piece of reportage. Look back again at Mrs Bishop's account of the sinking of *The Titanic* from her view in a lifeboat. Imagine that you are one of the passengers stranded on the upper deck as the ship sinks. Write a personal account of the main events as you see them. Use the same time period as the one covered by Mrs Bishop in her account: from the time that the bow section started to sink below the surface, to the stern rising up vertically and the ship sinking quickly beneath the sea. As you write, think about:

● the person (first, second or third) you write in
● the tone of voice which you use, e.g. happy, sad, frightened, angry, calm
● your choice of language in order to hold the interest of the reader
● where you are in relation to the incident (on the upper deck) and how this affects what you see and experience
● the situation of the other passengers and how they react
● what thoughts and feelings you were experiencing during the period that the incident took place.

Remember that this was an actual event that took place and that you are trying to write a truthful and accurate account from your personal experience. Try to avoid making things up unnecessarily.

Review

In this unit you have learned the main features of the type of personal account writing known as reportage. This type of writing involves a closeness of the writer to the event being recorded, in much the same way that a live TV programme might record an important event, such as a royal wedding or funeral. But of course, print reportage is not visual like a camera, and this inevitably affects the tone and the style of writing used, in order to bring the events alive in the mind of the reader.

'Out damned spot!'

Aims

- To learn about the language of persuasion. Much of the persuasive language which we come across appears in advertisements selling products.

Starter session

Work with a partner. Each of you should try to think of an advert which has made a lasting impression on you. This advert can be either from television or from the magazines that you read for enjoyment. Try to note down everything that you can remember about the advert, under the following headings:

- The product being advertised
- Exactly why it stuck in your mind
  - Was it the people shown in the advert?
  - Were there any memorable images or pictures used?
  - Were there were any particular words or phrases which stood out?

Swap with your partner and take turns to read each other's notes. From what you know, does your partner's description of their chosen advert seem accurate?

Introduction

The language of persuasion as it appears in adverts is all around us.

- As we watch TV (other than the BBC) our programmes are regularly interrupted to sell us a vast range of products, from chocolate to the latest motor car.
- As we travel to school by car or bus, we pass roadside billboards advertising the latest Playstation game, or perhaps even another TV programme.

- As we read our favourite newspaper or magazine, we are asked to consider the latest personal computer or mobile phone.

What all of these advertising situations have in common, however, is that they use language to try and **persuade** us to buy the product on offer. In the case of printed media (newspapers and magazines) the language is written down, whereas in the case of visual and sound media (TV and radio), the language is mainly spoken. The best examples of advertising tend to combine the use of both language and pictures.

For example, there is an advert on TV for Levi jeans which shows a young man and a woman side-by-side, indoors, racing each other. As the advert develops, they repeatedly 'crash through the walls of the house' until they eventually spill out into outer space. On the face of it, it is difficult to see how the action is connected to the product being sold – Levi jeans. The images used are certainly very striking. But on reflection, perhaps it is trying to say something along the lines that:

- Levi jeans appeal to young, competitive people
- Levi jeans allow us to break down all sorts of barriers which face us – mental and physical
- Levi jeans will eventually allow us to be free and unhindered.

The vivid images are also reinforced by the words 'Levis: The Freedom to Move'.

Development

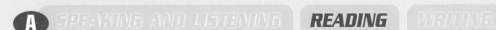

A SPEAKING AND LISTENING **READING** WRITING

Look carefully at the advert opposite and answer the following questions:
- Is it clear from a first reading what is being advertised?
- Do you think that this was written to appeal to young boys or girls? Give reasons for your answers.
- What is your instant reaction to the advert? Is it positive or negative?
- Does the advert make you want to know more about the product?

YOU DON'T NEED A LOT OF TACKLE

YOU NEED ONE THAT TACKLES THE LOT

WHEN YOU HAVE A **SPOT OF BOTHER** WITH THE OLD BOD. WHAT DO YOU TURN TO - AN ARMY FROM THE PHARMACY - OR **NATURE'S REVENGE!** TEA TREE OIL IS PROBABLY THE MOST **POWERFUL NATURAL ANTISEPTIC** KNOWN TO MAN SO NEXT TIME YOU'RE BITTEN OR SMITTEN WITH AN IRRITATING OUTBREAK YOU WISH WOULD GO AWAY YOU KNOW THE ONE YOU WANT.

TEA TREE OIL FROM **AUSTRALIAN BODYCARE**

Look carefully again at the two pieces of headline writing in block capital letters:

YOU DON'T NEED A LOT OF TACKLE

YOU NEED ONE THAT TACKLES THE LOT

- Which is the key word in these two headlines and what effect does it have?

- Read closely the writing which appears in the shape that looks like a bookmark. Try to identify at least three examples of individual words or phrases which have been chosen to try and persuade you to buy this product. Say why you think they have been included. For example:
  - e.g. the phrase 'a spot of bother' plays on the fact that the product is aimed at getting rid of skin 'spots'
  - 'a spot of bother' is also a well-known phrase for 'trouble' which would be used and recognised by young people.

Advertising is big business. Most adverts are produced by specialists at advertising agencies who are experts in the language of persuasion, and they charge their clients – businesses which want to increase their sales – millions of pounds to produce adverts for a vast range of products.

You are now going to try and produce your own piece of persuasive writing. Split into groups of five or six. For each group:

● Imagine that you work for an advertising agency and that you have been approached by a company to produce an advert for one of its products.

● The task of each group is to produce the written brief or script for a one-minute advert to be broadcast on commercial TV.

● The following issues will need to be covered:
  - what product you are going to advertise
  - who you are trying to persuade to buy this product – the target audience
  - the 'story' which will be included in the advert
  - the setting (where the 'story' takes place) and any props required (including the product itself)
  - the characters to be included
  - the words to be spoken by each character
  - the directions involved
  - a phrase or slogan which sums up what you are trying to say in your advert.

● To clarify all of the above, you should try to 'storyboard' the advert – break the action down into scenes and draw rough sketches of each – as you go along.

Review

In this unit you have learnt how adverts appeal to their target audiences through a combination of carefully chosen language (spoken and written) and images (still and moving).

Down and out...

Aims

- To learn about the documentary style of writing. As the name suggests, this type of writing documents or records events, sometimes, but not always, from the point of view of the writer.

Starter session

Think about what goes on in your school from the time that you arrive in the morning until the time that you leave in the afternoon. Break the day down into time slots and record these on the board, for example:

8:40am	Arrive in school
8:55am	Registration
9:10am	First lesson

and so on…

Starting with the first time slot, a member of the class should stand up and describe in detail:

- what s/he did
- who s/he met and talked with.

When this person has finished s/he should nominate another member of the class to describe in detail what occurred in the next time period. Once all the time periods have been covered, go back to the beginning and start again.

Introduction

Documentary writing tries to give a detailed and truthful picture of an event or situation. As the name suggests, however, another main purpose of this style of writing is to serve as an accurate **document** or **record** of these events. This record can then be read by other individuals to get some idea of what actually happened in any particular event or situation.

Historians rely heavily on documentary writing to accurately re-tell the events of the past. For example, the letters written by soldiers in the First World War form an accurate and first-hand record of the awful conditions of war and life in the trenches. These letters are an important source of documentary writing for historians, and other people who give us a picture of past events.

Development

A SPEAKING AND LISTENING **READING** WRITING

Look at the extract below which is taken from George Orwell's autobiographical documentary *Down and Out in Paris and London*. This book records a period of his life spent amongst the poor of London and Paris. This particular extract describes the events surrounding the author's first visit to a pawn shop, to exchange some of his clothes and a suitcase in return for money.

As you read, think about:

● the amount of detail which Orwell goes into

● whether this level of detail makes the account either more or less realistic

● the use of relatively short sentences and whether this makes it easier or more difficult to understand.

ONE DAY my English lessons ceased abruptly. The weather was getting hot and one of my pupils, feeling too lazy to go on with his lessons, dismissed me. The other disappeared from his lodgings without notice; owing me twelve francs. I was left with only thirty centimes and no tobacco. For a day and a half I had nothing to eat or smoke, and then, too hungry to put it off any longer, I packed my remaining clothes into my suitcase and took them to the pawnshop. This put an end to all the pretence of being in funds, for I could not take my clothes out of the hotel without asking Madame F.'s leave. I remember, however, how surprised she was at my asking her instead of removing the clothes on the sly, shooting the moon being a common trick in our quarter.

It was the first time that I had been into a French pawnshop. One went through grandiose stone portals (marked, of course, 'Liberté, Egalité, Fraternité' – they write that even over the police stations in France) into a large

[continued over page]

bare room like a school classroom, with a counter and rows of benches. Forty or fifty people were waiting. One handed one's pledge over the counter and sat down. Presently, when the clerk had assessed its value, he would call out, '*Numero*such and such, will you take fifty francs?' Sometimes it was only fifteen francs, or ten, or five – whatever it was, the whole room knew it. As I came in the clerk called with an air of offence, '*Numero 83* – here!' and gave a little whistle and a beckon, as though calling a dog. *Numero 83* stepped to the counter; he was an old bearded man, with an overcoat buttoned up at the neck and frayed trouser-ends. Without a word the clerk shot the bundle across the counter – evidently it was worth nothing. It fell to the ground and came open, displaying four pairs of men's woollen pants. No one could help laughing. Poor *Numero 83* gathered up his pants and shambled out, muttering to himself.

The clothes I was pawning, together with the suitcase, had cost over twenty pounds, and were in good condition. I thought they must be worth ten pounds, and a quarter of this (one expects quarter value at a pawnshop) was two hundred and fifty or three hundred francs. I waited without anxiety, expecting two hundred francs at the worst.

At last the clerk called my number: '*Numero 97!*'

'Yes,' I said, standing up.

'Seventy francs?'

Seventy francs for ten pounds' worth of clothes! But it was no use arguing; I had seen someone else attempt to argue, and the clerk had instantly refused the pledge. I took the money and the pawnticket and walked out. I had now no clothes except what I stood up in – the coat badly out at elbow – an overcoat, moderately pawnable, and one spare shirt. Afterwards, when it is too late, I learned that it is wiser to go to a pawnshop in the afternoon. The clerks are French, and, like most French people, are in a bad temper till they have eaten their lunch.

When I got home, Madame F. was sweeping the bistro floor. She came up the steps to meet me. I could see in her eye that she was uneasy about my rent.

'Well,' she said, 'what did you get for your clothes? Not much, eh?'

'Two hundred francs,' I said promptly.

'*Tiens!*' she said, surprised; 'well, *that's* not bad. How expensive those English clothes must be!'

When you have finished reading the extract, think about the following:

- Did Orwell really have to live amongst the poor, to produce an accurate record of the dreadful conditions of the time?
- Could he have produced as accurate a picture, if he simply spent some time with them as an 'outside observer'?
- Are there any clues in the extract to tell you whether Orwell was either sympathetic or hostile towards the poor?
- Why you think Orwell felt the need to highlight the conditions of poverty in London and Paris in the 1930s?

You are now going to try and produce your own piece of documentary writing to be included in the school magazine.

- Choose a member of the school staff, e.g.
  - your English teacher
  - the Deputy Headteacher
  - the school Secretary
  - the caretaker
  - a dinner lady

or anyone else whose day you think it might be interesting to document.

- Your piece should be entitled 'A Day in the Life of.....'.
- Because your piece will be about someone else's day, it should be written in the third person. How does this differ from the Orwell extract?
- In order to complete this task you will have to get the permission of the individual whose day you wish to record.
- You will have to 'shadow' the person for as much of the day as possible, making detailed notes of everything that happens to them.
- Be prepared to ask questions of the person you have chosen, to understand what is happening and how they feel about things.

Before you begin, re-read the Orwell extract to remind you of his direct style and try to copy this style in your own piece of writing.

Review

In this unit you have learnt about the main features of documentary writing and why it is important to keep an accurate record of events and situations. You have also learnt that good documentary writing is written in a direct style and from a realistic point of view.

Print and be damned

Aims

- To learn about editorial writing in relation to newspapers.

Starter session

Discuss with a partner the names of all the daily and Sunday newspapers which you can think of. List them under two columns headed *Broadsheet* and *Tabloid*. If you are not sure which column some of them should be listed in, make a guess. Add a third column to record whether you think the political views of the paper are either right-wing (normally, close to the Conservative Party); or left-wing (normally, close to the Labour Party); or centre (normally, close to the Liberal Democrat Party). Again, if you are unsure, make a guess anyway.

Your teacher will gather information on the board from different pairs, and correct any mistakes. Be prepared to give reasons for your choices.

Introduction

One of the main purposes of newspapers is to report news as accurately as possible. In doing this, newspapers would argue that they try to be as objective, truthful and unbiased as they can. Another purpose of newspapers, however, is to give their own views on the news. These views appear most directly in a section known as the 'editorial'. The newspaper's views normally reflect the political views which it sympathises with. In many cases, these in turn reflect the views of those individuals or businesses which own the newspaper. For example, *The Sun*, a daily tabloid, has traditionally been a supporter of the Conservative Party and therefore, is seen to be right-wing. In turn, *The Sun* is owned by Rupert Murdoch, a multi-millionaire businessman, and traditional Conservative supporter, with well known right-wing views.

Development

SPEAKING AND LISTENING **READING** **WRITING**

Read the editorial printed below. It is from *The Mirror*, a daily tabloid. As you read make notes on the following questions:

- Why is *The Mirror* called a tabloid type of newspaper?
- What are the main differences between a tabloid and a broadsheet type of newspaper?
- Are there clues which tell you the political views of the paper – either right-wing, or left-wing, or centre?
- How much does the editorial tell you about the facts of each piece?
- Why do you think the three pieces have appeared in that particular order:
  - 1st – 'Euan Blair's right to private life'
  - 2nd – The rail solution
  - 3rd – Force of hobbit?
- In what way does the final piece try to be humorous? Why do you think this attempt at humour was made?
- Why have different fonts and styles been used throughout the editorial?

VOICE OF THE Mirror

We respect Euan's right to private life

JUST because Euan Blair is the Prime Minister's son does not mean he has to live his whole life in the public eye.

So it was right for the Press Complaints Commission to condemn two newspapers which revealed details of his university application.

[continued over page]

The situation of young people who are the children of the famous has been made very clear by the PCC.

The principle was laid down for the sake of Princes William and Harry but it should apply to all in their position.

Few young people would want to have their applications for university publicised. That would make them feel a greater failure if they did not manage to get in.

Yet it is ridiculous to suggest that just because Euan went to a film premiere, open season can be declared on his private life.

The PCC does not demand that young people must live the life of a monk unless they want everything they do to be reported and photographed.

The Blairs have been rigid in protecting their children. Most parents would feel the same in their situation.

Youngsters deserve the chance to grow up as normally as possible, whatever their parents do.

There can be advantages in being the child of someone famous.

But there can also be disadvantages and they should not be made worse by being exposed to public scrutiny.

The rail solution

THE battle to sort out the railways is going to need the support of everyone who works on them.

Strikes are only adding to the crisis. And so is strike-breaking by managers.

Train passengers have been incredibly tolerant of the stoppages, which are currently hitting South West Trains.

But you need to be tolerant to travel on the railways. When you regularly have to put up with delays, cancellations and dreadful service, a few strikes are hardly noticeable.

The task for everyone involved with the railways – from government, through train firms, managers, drivers, guards and station staff – is to work together to sort out the chaos.

Bosses and unions need to solve their differences so they can get on with the real problems.

Force of hobbit

IN the great battle of the Baftas, the hobbits have leapt into the lead.

The Lord Of The Rings has received 13 nominations to eight for its great rival, Harry Potter.

But there is hope for the young wizard of Hogwarts. He may yet master the darkest art of all – getting nominated for the Oscars.

B SPEAKING AND LISTENING   READING   **WRITING**

You are now going to try and produce your own piece of editorial writing.

- Imagine that you are the editor of the school newspaper, with the specific job of writing the editorial section.

- Identify an important issue which is being discussed widely in school. This can either be a real issue or one that you make up, for example:
  - the compulsory wearing of school uniform
  - the proposal to sell off the school playing fields to build houses
  - the need for tighter security to prevent strangers from entering the school buildings and grounds.
  (These are only suggestions. If you have a better one of your own, choose it.)

- Using ICT, if possible, try to write your editorial in the style of *The Mirror*:
  - using a variety of different fonts and styles
  - using persuasive language
  - clearly stating your (or the school newspaper's) views on the matter.

Review

In this unit you have learnt that writing newspaper editorials involves:

- expressing a clear point of view usually reflecting the political views of the paper and its owners
- using persuasive rather than neutral language
- using an opinionated rather than objective style.

'Giga bytes Mac and crashes'

Aims

- To learn about how the growth of information and computer technology has affected certain aspects of the English language.

Starter session

ICT has made an enormous impact on all of our lives in recent years, and has led to massive changes in the way that we communicate, work and play. Computers are the most obvious example of the growth of ICT, but there are hosts of others. Try to think of some. When you have done so, raise your hand and give your example to the rest of the class. Try also to say what the example is used for, for instance a PC (personal computer) could be used for writing up your homework, logging onto the Internet, and so on.Once a member of the class has successfully given an example and description, s/he should nominate someone else to give the next example.

Introduction

As ICT spreads, it affects the language which we use, especially as new terms and words are introduced to describe and talk about the new technology. Some of these terms might be specialist terms, e.g.

- 'MHz' which is an abbreviation of 'Megahertz', the speed at which computers work.

Others have become part of our everyday speech, e.g.

- *PC* – personal computer
- *software* – computer programs and applications which allow us to use a computer

Development

Read the article below which is taken from a recent copy of a monthly computer magazine published in the UK. The article refers to the sales launch of a new version of the iMac computer produced by the computer firm Apple. As you read the article, write down all the words, terms and phrases which relate to ICT. Some of them you may already understand, but some of them you may not.

APPLE UNVEILS NEW iMAC

The Macworld expo in San Francisco saw the dawn of another new era for the Macintosh. In his keynote speech on 7th January, Apple CEO Steve Jobs announced new software and a new version of the company's popular iBook laptop. Most significantly, though, there will also be a brand new version of the best-selling iMac.

The iMac has been completely redesigned. The new model has a 15" LCD panel, and users will have the choice of a G4 processor running at either 700MHz or 800MHz. The all-in-one design features a hemispherical base containing the motherboard, disc drives and power supply, which connects to the display via a 'neck' that makes it look as if the screen is floating.

[continued over page]

Since the beginning of 2001, Apple has been positioning its computers as the 'digital hub' – the central component of 'digital lifestyle' accessories such as MP3 players, camcorders and DVD players. As part of MacOS, the company already provides iTunes for MP3 recording and playback, iMovie for digital video editing and iDVD for DVD authoring on high-end Macs equipped with a DVD writer. During his speech, Jobs introduced the fourth component of this software strategy: iPhoto. This program allows users to download images from digital still cameras, crop them, store them, print them and publish them on a website. Although all this has been possible in the past, iPhoto simplifies the entire process and adds extra features such as the ability to order Kodak prints of digital images online at up to 20x30".

Working with a partner, arrange the words and phrases into a table with columns as shown below (the first few ICT terms have been identified to get you started):

Word, Term, Phrase	Meaning	Everyday	Specialist
Macintosh			
software			
laptop			
iMac			
15" LCD panel			

Discuss the list with your partner.

- Say whether you think that the word, term or phrase is part of our everyday language, or is a 'specialist' term which would only be used in relation to ICT.
- Try to discover the meaning of the terms which you have identified. Re-read the article and look at where the term appears. It might be that this will help you to make a reasonable guess about the meaning of some of the terms. Alternatively, you may have to visit the library (either in school, or your local library) to look up the meaning of the terms in an ICT specialist dictionary. If you cannot get hold of an ICT dictionary, you might be able to talk to the teacher in your school who is responsible for ICT.

Text messaging on mobile phones is yet another example of ICT which is on the increase, especially amongst young people. It seems that a whole new language is emerging for texting, with:

● new words – sometimes combining numbers and letters

● new phrases – sometimes abbreviations of longer phrases

● and pictures/images

becoming more widespread and commonly used.

Why do you think this 'new language' for text messaging has come about?

Study the three text messages which appear below. Working on your own, see if you can translate them into standard written English – the normal way that you would write about things in your English class.

1
> Hi ya! RUOK?
> Still going 2 d
> concert 2ngt?
> CU l8r.

2
> RU in skool
> 2day? I'm
> feeling bad,
> sick L fone U l8r.

3
> fancy goin
> shopping 2ngt?
> Need a new top
> 4 hot d8 at...

> ...wkend. can't
> w8! Ded
> excited J let
> me know wot
> time Byeeee!

Review

In this unit you have learnt that ICT has made a massive impact not only on our everyday and working lives, but also on the language which we use to communicate. It is important to note that language has always changed as new developments and technology have spread, and therefore, the spread of ICT and its impact on the language is nothing new. Our language is constantly changing as new words, usually starting off as specialist words, gradually become more and more accepted and commonly used.

Travel by dhow

Aims

- To learn about one type of **journal writing**, kept to record the details of a journey.

Starter session

Study the list below and answer the questions which follow:

> woke late for school   in trouble with teacher
>
> met with friends for lunch   text messaged Sophie with latest news
>
> my final memory of you   missed last bus home.

- Are any of the above proper sentences?
- Do they make sense as they read?
- Have you come across this style of writing before? If so, say where.
- To make them into proper sentences what would you have to do? Try to re-write them as proper sentences.

Introduction

Travel writing is a popular type of non-fiction writing. As people travel, many like to keep a written record of the people, events and situations that they come into contact with. They might keep these details in the form of a daily diary or journal. Journals can be kept for a variety of reasons:

- simply as a personal record or **memoire** for the interest of the person writing the journal
- in the case of travel writing, to record for academic purposes, the experiences of travelling to unfamiliar and perhaps unusual places
- for the purpose of entertainment – given that much travel writing can be very funny.

In addition to these reasons, the purpose of a journal is to make the reader aware of the writer's thoughts and feelings as s/he travels.

Development

Read the extract below. It is taken from a travel book *Around the World in 80 Days* by the ex-Monty Python comedian, Michael Palin, and was also a successful BBC TV travel series. The book and the TV programme are named after a similarly titled novel written by Jules Verne in 1873. In both the original and modern versions, the main story concerns an attempt (one imaginary and one real) to try and travel around the world in 80 days.
As you read, think about the following:

- Look carefully at some of the sentences which the author uses, e.g. the first sentence: 'Woken from a five-hour sleep by the sound of a telephone at my bedside.'

- What is unusual about this sentence?

- Can you identify other examples of sentences where there appear to be some words missing?

- What effect do these **minor sentences** (sometimes also called **elliptical** sentences) have on you as you read them?

- Do they make the extract easier or more difficult to understand?

- Is this extract written in a serious or humorous tone of voice? Can you give at least one example to support your view?

**DAY 16
10 OCTOBER**

Woken from a five-hour sleep by the sound of a telephone at my bedside. Good news and bad news. The good news is that we have secured a dhow to take us to Bombay. The bad news is that it leaves at dawn tomorrow. No time for recovery before a six-day voyage on an open boat. On the other hand the sooner we move on the better. I must not forget that Phileas Fogg, aboard the *Mongolia* all the way, reached Bombay in eighteen days.

Walk out onto the quayside. My first sight of a dhow. Only nostalgic, crossword-loving Western romantics still call them dhows. To the locals they are 'launches' or 'coastal vessels'. They are wooden, built to a traditional design resembling in shape a slice of melon, with a high stern on which sits the wheelhouse, a draught of 15 or 20 feet, and a length of about 60 feet.

[continued over page]

There seems to be no shortage of them in Dubai. There are twenty or thirty lined up in this inlet of the river they call The Creek. One is loading crates of 'Tiger's Head' brand flashlights, made in China, 'Coast' full-cream milk powder, boxes of Tide washing powder, 'White Elephant' dry battery cells, Sanyo radios and a twin-tub washing machine. Its destination is Berbera in Somalia.

Every one of the dhows is like a floating small business, and generally run by family and friends, though owned, as likely as not, by some shrewd import-exporter in a stretch Mercedes. They present quite a different dockside ambiance from any I've experienced so far. Instead of cranes and gantries and hard-hats and bulk loads and lorries, operating behind guardposts and fences, the dhows are serviced, right in the centre of town, by small pick-up trucks, trolleys and men's backs. People bustle around, scrambling over the boats like ants, arranging, moving, heaving and hoisting the cargo. The reason for the great activity at the moment is that these are some of the first boats out after the monsoon season from May to August, during which the dhows are laid up because of storms.

In the afternoon we are taken by Kamis, an agent for the port and customs department to see the boat that will be our home for the next week. The M.V. *Al Sharma* (meaning 'Candlelight') is a trim, freshly-painted ship, and her Captain, Hassan Syleyman, bounds across the deckful of date sacks to welcome us. He smiles broadly and constantly, especially when giving us bad news, so it is a moment before it sinks in that he is telling us he will not be leaving tomorrow, but the next day, Wednesday, 12 October. Day 18.

All the time made up on the hectic scramble from Jeddah is suddenly lost again, but there is nothing we can do. Clem disappears to have words with the owners, Nigel and the other Passepartouts to the other end of the quay to film. I'm left with the taxi drivers. One nods towards the *Al Shamra*. 'You go on that?' He clearly can't believe it. The other joins in. 'These boats no restaurant!' He shakes his head vigorously, mistaking my smile for disbelief. 'No clean, nowhere sleep!' Now they both shake their heads, like witches. 'It will be six, seven days, you know. Terrible…Terrible! Three days on a dhow, fifteen in hospital!'

In the afternoon we are taken by Kamis, an agent for the port and customs department to see the boat that will be our home for the next week. The M.V. *Al Sharma* (meaning 'Candlelight') is a trim, freshly-painted ship, and her Captain, Hassan Syleyman, bounds across the deckful of date sacks to welcome us. He smiles broadly and constantly, especially when giving us bad news, so it is a moment before it sinks in that he is telling us he will not be leaving tomorrow, but the next day, Wednesday, 12 October. Day 18.

All the time made up on the hectic scramble from Jeddah is suddenly lost again, but there is nothing we can do. Clem disappears to have words with the owners, Nigel and the other Passepartouts to the other end of the quay to film. I'm left with the taxi drivers. One nods towards the *Al Sharma*. 'You go on that?' He clearly can't believe it. The other joins in. 'These boats no restaurant!' He shakes his head vigorously, mistaking my smile for disbelief. 'No clean, nowhere sleep!' Now they both shake their heads, like witches. 'It will be six, seven days, you know. Terrible…Terrible! Three days on a dhow, fifteen in hospital!'

You are now going to try and produce a piece of journal writing of your own. Think back to a journey that you have made in the past. It need not be as glamorous as the round-the-world trip referred to above, although it could be a holiday that you have had abroad. It could equally, however, be a journey that you have made in this country. For the purposes of this task, you are allowed on occasion to 'stretch the truth'.

Write up the journal entry for three days of the journey, one following on from the other. As you write, remember the following:

● try to keep the interest of the audience, by perhaps concentrating on any unusual occurrences

● adopt a style which lets the reader feel that s/he is actually there with you on the journey

● use a specific tone of voice – either sad or humorous – depending on the situation.

Review

In this unit you have learnt about one type of travel writing – that involving the keeping of a journal. This type of writing, as well as informing you about the journey being made and entertaining you, also tries to 'draw you in' to the journey, to give the impression that you are actually there with the writer.

Up, up and away

Aims

● To learn about writing that is largely technical and specific.

Starter session

Many, if not all of you, will have flown in an aeroplane. But even if you haven't, you will be aware of many details about aeroplanes and air flight. Think carefully about what you do know.

● Identify a word or term relating to aeroplanes and air flight, that you are familiar with.

● When you have thought of one, come out to the front and write it on the board.

● When you have written it, turn round to the rest of the class and say what it means.

● Your teacher will nominate someone to check the spelling of your word or phrase in the dictionary.

● See if you can get around the whole class before you run out of ideas.

● The following are provided to get you started:

aeroplane   propeller   air traffic control

landing gear   cabin crew   helicopter

Introduction

In our everyday lives we come across a range of complex technological processes, most of which we take for granted such as:

● an alarm clock   ● boiling an egg   ● getting hot water from a shower
● getting to school by car or bus   ● riding your bike
● getting a hot school meal for lunch

Think about the chair that you are currently sitting on. On the face of it, your chair is a simple, everyday item. But think of the time and effort which must have gone into its design and manufacture, to make sure that you can sit comfortably, whilst it takes your weight. Even the most simple examples of technology, therefore, can require detailed, and often complex, explanation.

Development

A   SPEAKING AND LISTENING   **READING**   WRITING

Read the extract below which gives information on how light aircraft fly. This sort of information would normally appear in books like encyclopedias, or even technical instruction manuals. As you read, think about the ways in which the author makes a difficult technological process easy to understand, in particular:
– look at the sentence structure – what can you say about the length of the sentences used?
– what purpose does the inclusion of the section 'Making Lift' have, in terms of the extract as a whole?

LIGHT AIRCRAFT

THE BODY OF AN aeroplane is called the fuselage. Most small planes – called light aircraft – are pushed through the air by propellers turned at high speed by powerful engines. There is a variety of moveable control surfaces on the aeroplane. Ailerons on the main wings help an aeroplane to roll or bank (tilt to the side) into a turn. The rudder on the aeroplane's fin (tail) is used to steer left or right. The elevators on the tailplane make the plane climb or descend.

As the wing moves through the air, it splits the air in two. Air that passes over the wing moves faster than air that passes below it, because the upper surface is more curved. This shape is known as the aerofoil section. The fast-moving air produces less pressure on the upper wing surface than the slower-moving air underneath. So there is an overall upwards push – lift. The amount of lift depends on the speed the aeroplane moves, the area of the wings, and the curvature of the aerofoil section. Heavy aeroplanes, such as jumbo jets, need large wings and powerful jet engines to push them through the air quickly enough.

Making lift

How can you make a piece of paper rise without touching it to push it upwards? Cut out a strip of paper about 3cm wide and 15cm long. Hold one end of the strip between one finger and the thumb of each hand, just in front of and below your bottom lip. Now blow over the top of the paper, and you will see it lift into the air. As you blow, you are creating fast-moving air over the paper, like the air passing over the top of a wing. The still air underneath the paper pushes upwards more than the faster-moving air above the paper pushes downwards, lifting the paper.

B SPEAKING AND LISTENING   READING   **WRITING**

You are now going to try and produce your own piece of writing, explaining a technological process.

Choose one example of technology. You might like to look back to the Introduction section earlier in the lesson. Alternatively, you might like to choose another example which you are more familiar with. The example which you choose can either be a complex or simple example – the choice is yours!

Your task is to write an explanation, in the style of the extract above, of the technological processes involved in the example which you have chosen. When writing, remember to:

- cover as much detail as you can
- pay attention to the length and structure of your sentences, to ensure clarity
- include any illustrations or diagrams which you are able to produce and which might help the reader to understand the explanation you are giving
- give any simple examples.

If you are stuck, you might find help by either consulting an encyclopedia, or if possible, getting information from the Internet.

Review

In this unit you have learnt about how to produce an explanation of a relatively complex technological process, so that it can be understood by someone who might know very little about the subject.

'Humdinger'

Aims

● To learn another way to write about a complex technological process.

Starter session

Work with a partner. Look at the six simple sentences below.

1 The dog chased the cat.
2 I was so tired.
3 My sister was taken ill.
4 The teacher shouted at the class.
5 The school bus was late.
6 I enjoyed the lesson.

With your partner, you should try to convert these simple sentences into complex sentences by adding words, phrases and clauses. You should take turns in making the additions. An example, using the first sentence, is given below to help you.

● The dog chased the cat.

● The lively dog chased the dozing cat.

● The lively dog which was looking for some excitement, chased the dozing cat around the kitchen.

● The lively dog which was looking for some excitement to relieve its boredom, chased the dozing ginger tom cat around the kitchen and created havoc.

And so on…

When you have finished, raise your hand and read out one of your complex sentences to the rest of the class. Your teacher will judge how successful you have been.

Introduction

Non-fiction writing can be split into two broad types:

Non-literary non-fiction

● The main focus of this type of writing is to inform, explain, describe, persuade, analyse or argue in a very direct style. The writing tends to be direct, to the point and written in straightforward, simple language.

Literary non-fiction

● The main focus of this type of writing is to be imaginative and perhaps even entertaining, whilst at the same time trying to provide information. The writing tends to be much more 'literary' in style, and uses techniques more normally found in fiction:
  – referring to characters
  – trying to create a story
  – using figurative language to create pictures in the mind of the reader
  – being conscious of the tone of voice adopted to maintain the interest of the reader.

It is possible, however, that these two very different styles or **genres** of writing can be used to cover the same general subject matter, both informing, but in very different ways, and appealing to different audiences.

Development

 SPEAKING AND LISTENING **READING** WRITING

Read the extract opposite, explaining how the hummingbird flies and answer the questions which follow. It was written by David Attenborough, a well-known writer on the natural world. Notice that although the subject is similar, the style of writing is very different to the description of aircraft flight in Unit 8. The subject is still flight. But in this instance you are looking at how birds fly, not humans in aircraft.

THE MASTERY OF FLIGHT

ONLY ONE FAMILY OF BIRDS can truly hover in still air for any length of time. They are the hummingbirds. They need to do so in order to hang in front of a flower while they perform the delicate task of inserting their slim sharp bills into its depths to drink nectar. Their thin wings are not contoured into the shape of aerofoils and do not generate lift in this way. Their flying technique differs from that of most other birds' as radically as helicopters do from fixed-wing aircraft.

The long bones of their wings have been greatly reduced in length, and the joints at the wrist and the elbow have lost nearly all their mobility. Their paddle-shaped wings are, in effect, hands that swivel at the shoulder. They beat them in such a way that the tip of each wing follows the line of a figure-of-eight, lying on its side. The wing moves forward and downwards into the front loop of the eight, creating lift. As it begins to come up and goes back, the wing twists through 180 degrees so that once again it creates a downward thrust. If the lift produced on each loop of the figure-of-eight is equally strong, the bird will remain stationary in the air. A slight alteration in the twist, changing the angle at which the wing moves downward, is enough to move the bird forwards – or even backwards.

This manner of flying demands a great deal of energy. Nectar, the hummingbird's food, is the biological equivalent of high-octane fuel but even so a hummingbird consumes such quantities that it may need to refuel as many as two thousand times a day. Even at rest its body needs a great deal of fuel simply to keep ticking over. Part of this is used to keep its flying muscles at a high temperature and ready for instant take-off. But when night comes and it is unable to see to fly, those muscles are not used and that heat is not needed. So in the evening when a hummingbird arrives on its roost, it deliberately ruffles its feathers and allows its body to cool. During the day, its heart beats between five hundred and twelve hundred times a second. Now it slows down so much that its throb is virtually undetectable. Nor does the bird appear to be breathing. In effect, it is doing what a hedgehog does when winter approaches. It is hibernating. A hummingbird, however, has to hibernate three hundred and sixty five times every year.

- In what ways is this extract similar to the extract in the previous unit (Unit 8)?

- In what ways, however, do you think that it differs? Think carefully about the language used. For example, compare these two sentences:
  - 'Heavy aeroplanes, such as jumbo jets, need large wings and powerful jet engines to push them through the air quickly.' (Unit 8)
  - 'Nectar, the hummingbird's food, is the biological equivalent of high-octane fuel but even so a hummingbird consumes such quantities that it may need to refuel as many as two thousand times a day.' (Unit 9)

  List the differences between them.

Both articles deal with the complex technological process of flight.

- Which of the two extracts explains the process of flight the best? Give reasons for your answer.
- The hummingbird extract uses figurative language to sustain your interest. Can you find examples of this type of language? Here is one to get you started: 'paddle-shaped wings'.
- One of these extracts also featured in a BBC television programme. By comparing the way that the two articles are written, could you guess which of the two it is? Give reasons for your answer.

B SPEAKING AND LISTENING   READING   **WRITING**

You are now going to try and produce your own piece of writing on a complex technological process, in the style of the extract on the hummingbird.

A bicycle, believe it or not, works according to a set of a fairly complex technological principles and actions, but the basic steps in the process are as follows:

- a human body provides power by turning the pedals
- the pedals are connected through a series of gears to the rear wheel
- the rear wheels turn on the road's surface and the bicycle moves forward.

Try to visualise these steps in your mind before you begin to write. Can you think of any of the other steps in between these main ones? You should try to bring the image of the cyclist riding her/his bicycle to life, by:

- Writing in the third person (using the pronoun he. she or it)
- Using the present tense (to make it feel that the action is really happening)
- Using lots of figurative language, imagery, metaphors and similes, to describe the action
- Varying the length of sentences to maintain interest
- Imagining that you are writing your explanation as part of a script for a television programme.

Review

In this unit you have learned that not all complex technological processes need be explained in a direct, matter-of-fact way. Both the extract on air flight and the extract on the hummingbird are about the process of flight, but the hummingbird piece is written in a more 'literary', imaginative style. Both extracts, however, are equally effective, depending on why they were written and their intended audience.

'The Reds' vs 'The Reds'

Aims

● To learn about the importance of combining pictures and words to produce a commentary on an event.

Starter session

Work in groups of five or six. Your teacher will put on your desk a newspaper photograph or photographs of a recent event

Your task as a group is to produce a commentary on the photograph(s) in no more than 100 words. Someone from the group should be chosen to read it out to the rest of the class. In speaking you should refer back to the photo(s) to maintain interest in your talk.

Introduction

A lot of the non-fiction we read consists not only of written words, but also of pictures or images. Think of the following examples:

● newspapers   ● magazines   ● school textbooks
● leaflets   ● web pages from the Internet

Pictures added to writing often help us to get a better idea of what is going on in a text. For example, the biggest news story of 2001 was probably the terrorist attack on the World Trade Centre in New York on 11 September.

Imagine if there had been no images available of this tragedy. What impact would this have had on newspaper and magazine coverage? Is there a difference between the impact of still pictures and moving images (particularly 'live' images) when reporting news events?

Development

SPEAKING AND LISTENING **READING** WRITING

Look at the article which appears below. It is a sports commentary on a football match, taken from the BBC Online website.

- What, if anything, do you think the pictures add to the writing?
- Is there a purpose to where the pictures are placed in the article?
- Would any other pictures have added to the impact of the writing? If so, which other pictures you would have liked to have seen included?
- Is the report balanced and objective, or can you detect any bias on the part of the writer? Give examples from the article.
- Do you think that the fact that this was an article on a website affected the way it was presented and laid out?
- Are there any obvious clues in the writing which identify it as a website article, rather than one which appeared in a newspaper?
- Do you think reading this sort of report on a website has any advantages over listening to it on the radio or watching it on live TV? Give reasons for your answer.

BBC SPORT

Front Page
Football
Statistics
FA Cup
Eng Prem
World Cup 2002
Champions League
Uefa Cup
Worthington Cup
Eng Div 1
Eng Div 2
Eng Div 3
Eng Conf
Scot Prem
Scottish Cup
CIS Ins Cup
Scot Div 1

You are in: Football

Liverpool's famous five

It seems there is never a bad time for the modern day Liverpool to play Manchester United.

Liverpool manager Gerard Houllier issued prophetic words as he swallowed the bitter disappointment of FA Cup defeat against Manchester United in 1999.

United scored two injury-time goals to beat Liverpool and Houllier insisted: 'One day we will beat Manchester United. I promise you that.'

He was right – although even he could not promise Liverpool would beat United five times in swift succession.

Danny Murphy's late goal made it a nap hand for Liverpool in recent meetings.

And while Liverpool may not have released Manchester United's stranglehold on the title, they have exercised complete mastery in head-to-head confrontations.

Murphy scored the winner in a single goal triumph at Old Trafford last season and repeated the dose to revive Liverpool's title bid this term.

Throw in two comfortable Anfield victories and a Charity Shield triumph, and the measure of Liverpool's supremacy in the games against their arch-rivals can be truly measured.

Sir Alex Ferguson said: 'It was the same last year. They just played the ball forward and hoped to get a break.'

This, of course, is nonsense.

Thompson banked on Liverpool's defence holding out, while hoping the pace of men like Michael Owen and latterly Nicolas Anelka, would help get a priceless goal.

It worked like a charm – and Ferguson, in his heart of hearts, will have to accept that it was a perfect counter-attacking thrust.

And United are past masters in the art of the counter-attack.

Liverpool's victories at Anfield, a 2–0 win last season and 3–1 in November, also proved there is more than one weapon to Liverpool's armoury.

United can rightly claim supremacy when it comes to trophies.

Ferguson's men rightly remain title favourites, but the law of averages dictated their run could not last forever.

And for those chasing the title – not only Liverpool but also Leeds United, Arsenal, Newcastle United and Chelsea – they have cause to be thankful to Danny Murphy.

You are now going to try and produce your own piece of commentary, combining writing and pictures.

● Your teacher will replay on the video recorder part of a sporting event – this may or may not be part of a football match.

● The video-recording will be no more than one minute long.

● You will not be able to hear the sound of the original commentator's voice.

Your task is to produce a written commentary on the video extract which you can then read out to the rest of the class. Make sure you include:

● some introductory remarks
  – what the event is
  – where it is taking place

● any relevant information which is not directly related to the action
  – some personal details about those sportswomen or sportsmen who are part of the action

● the detail of the action itself.

● a definite conclusion or summing up.

You will also need to think about your use of language. This becomes especially important when you are reading out your commentary. Think carefully about the tone and pace of delivery which you will need to use to make it interesting to listen to.

Review

In this unit you have learned how to combine writing with pictures to produce a commentary which holds the interest of the reader/viewer. You have done this in connection with a sporting event, but it could equally have applied to any news event or situation where pictures were available to support the writing. And even where no pictures exist, writing can be supported by other sorts of images, e.g. diagrams, sketches, 'artists' impressions' and so on.

American irony

Aims

● To learn about how writers use irony and sarcasm to make a piece of writing humorous and therefore enjoyable to read.

Starter session

Many of you will think that you are quite funny and have the ability to make others laugh. If you don't, then you will know of someone in the class who fits this bill; and, of course, there will be at least one resident class comedian!

Try to think of a funny remark or saying that you think the rest of the class will laugh at or find mildly amusing. When you have thought of one, raise your hand and tell it to the rest of the class. Once you have heard it, give it a score of between 1–10 to record how funny you think it was, with the most funny being 10 and the least funny being 1. Record on the board the names of those who made the remarks so that you eventually arrive at the Top Ten most amusing remarks.

In order to get you started here are three examples of what might be said.

1 Someone might say 'I'm going to play for England in the next World Cup.' To which someone else might respond 'And pigs might fly!'

2 Someone in the class might be well known for not liking English lessons and might say something like 'English is the best subject on our timetable – it's my absolute, all-time, one hundred percent, favourite subject…I don't think!'

3 Someone might be known for disliking the pop idol Will Young and might say 'Will Young is the greatest pop act since the break-up of Steps' (a double irony).

Introduction

We all say things we don't mean. Most of the time we say them by accident or in the heat of the moment and we have to apologise afterwards, e.g. during a heated argument you might say 'I hate you' to your brother or sister. You don't really hate them, and usually apologise later and make up. Quite often, however, we deliberately say things that we don't mean to try and add a touch of humour to our conversation. For example, in talking about your school, you might describe your teachers as being made up entirely of 'a strange collection of lunatics and weirdos'. Clearly, this is not the case in real life (at least one would hope that it wasn't!) but by describing them as such, it adds a touch of humour to the remark and adds to the overall interest of the conversation you might be having with your friends about school.

When we use words in a funny or mildly sarcastic or mocking way, to mean something different to their normal meaning (either in conversation or in our writing) we are using **irony**.

Much of the non-fiction writing that we come across is deliberately **ironic** in style in order to be funny, amusing and appealing to the reader.

Development

Look at the extract below. It is written by a well-known travel writer, Bill Bryson, who is famous for his use of irony and sarcasm in order to make his writing witty and humorous. Bryson, an American who came to Britain in his late teens, spent most of his 20s and 30s here, before eventually returning to the United States to live.

ONE

I come from Des Moines. Somebody had to.

When you come from Des Moines you either accept the fact without question and settle down with a local girl named Bobbi and get a job at the Firestone factory and live there for ever and ever, or you spend your adolescence moaning at length about what a dump it is and how you can't wait to get out, and then you settle down with a local girl named Bobbi and get a job at the Firestone factory and live there for ever and ever.

Hardly anyone ever leaves. This is because Des Moines is the most powerful hypnotic known to man. Outside town there is a big sign that says WECOME TO DES MOINES. THIS IS WHAT DEATH IS LIKE. There isn't really. I just made that up. But the place does get a grip on you. People who have nothing to do with Des Moines drive in off the interstate, looking for gas or hamburgers, and stay for ever. There's a New Jersey couple up the street from my parents' house whom you see wandering around from time to time looking faintly puzzled but strangely serene. Everybody in Des Moines is strangely serene.

The only person I ever knew in Des Moines who wasn't serene was Mr Piper. Mr Piper was my parents neighbour, a leering cherry-faced idiot who was forever getting drunk and crashing his car into telephone poles. Everywhere you went you encountered telephone poles and road signs leaning dangerously in testimony to Mr Piper's driving habits. He distributed them all over the west side of town, rather in the way dogs mark trees. Mr Piper was the nearest possible human equivalent to Fred Flintstone, but less charming. He appeared to feel he had a mission in life to spread offence. His favourite pastime, apart from getting drunk and crashing his car, was to get drunk and insult the neighbours.

Mr Piper is dead now, which is of course one thing that Des Moines prepares you for.

A SPEAKING AND LISTENING **READING** WRITING

After you have read the extract:

- Try to identify at least five examples of where Bryson is trying to be funny by his use of irony, for example 'I come from Des Moines. Somebody had to.' The second sentence is ironic because Bryson is trying to make a joke over and above the obvious statement that some people do come from Des Moines. The joke is that Des Moines is not really all that exciting a place for anyone to come from!

- Look at the examples which you have identified and try to explain the irony being used.

- A lot of Bryson's humour is also sarcastic. He deliberately mocks certain people or things. Can you identify any examples of sarcasm in the extract? Do you find his sarcasm humorous? Give reasons for your answer.

- Bryson is a travel writer. One of the main purposes of his writing is to inform us of places he has visited and the people and experiences he has encountered along the way.
  - Do you think that he can still inform us of these things whilst trying to be funny at the same time?
  - What do you think are the dangers involved in using humour as the main way of describing a piece of travel writing.

B SPEAKING AND LISTENING   READING   **WRITING**

Now you are going to try and produce your own piece of writing where irony is used to make the piece funny.

- Think about the street where you live and the neighbours you are surrounded by.
- Choose two or three individuals and describe:
  - what they look like
  - whether they have any peculiar habits
  - how they talk to you
  - what they think of you.
- It might be that the people that you choose are not really all that funny, but remember that the trick of writing in an ironic style is to say things which might have a different, exaggerated or opposite meaning to what they normally mean. In doing so, you might also have to exaggerate certain qualities of the people whom you are writing about.

As you write, try to copy Bryson's style of writing. You might need to keep referring to the extract to remind you of this.

Review

In this unit you have learnt:
- that humour can often be a very important part of non-fiction writing
- that in order to achieve this humour, many writers use irony
- what irony is and how it is created
- that there is sometimes a danger of humour getting in the way of another main purpose of the writing.

You tak' the high road...

Aims

● To learn that not all travel writing needs to be funny to be interesting. The use of a very formal style of writing using Standard English can perhaps be more informative and equally appealing.

Starter session

With a partner, look at the sentences which appear in the table below.

Colloquial sentence(s)	Standard English 'equivalent'
My throat is as dry as a bone. I could murder a cup of tea.	
The new Sony PlayStation 2 is boss, it's the business!	
Gareth Gates is fit – he can chill out with me anytime!	
	On Saturday nights I like to go out and have an evening's entertainment with my friends. We generally go to the cinema or to the local discotheque.
	My favourite teacher at school is Mrs Jones, the very experienced English teacher. She is an inspiration to us all and she makes the study of English extremely enjoyable.
	Whenever I am feeling sad and depressed, I contact my beloved on my mobile phone and send an affectionate text message.

- When 'translating' from the colloquial or slang to Standard English, think about how you would have to write down the sentence if you were writing it in an English examination.
- When 'translating' from Standard English to the colloquial, think about how you would normally say what is written, if you were talking amongst your friends.

When you and your partner have finished 'translating' these six examples, raise your hand and read one out to the rest of the class.

Introduction

Travel writing and travel writers come in many different styles. In the previous unit, we saw how Bill Bryson employs a very informal and humorous style of writing which relies on irony and sarcasm to grab the interest of the reader. Indeed, it could be argued that sometimes the humour of his writing tends to detract from his ability to give the reader information about his travels.

Many travel writers, however, write in a much more formal and less colloquial style than Bryson. It could be argued that the main purpose of such writers is to provide information about places, people and events to the reader in a straightforward manner, without the unnecessary distraction of making it funny in the process.

Development

Look at the extract opposite. It was written by James Boswell. Boswell is famous for his biography of his friend, Samuel Johnson – who is in turn famous for producing one of the first English dictionaries. The extract is in the form of a journal or diary, and describes part of a journey which both Boswell and Johnson made to the North-west Highlands of Scotland in 1773.

We had a very good ride for about three miles to Talisker, though we had showers from time to time. At Talisker, we found Mrs MacLeod, the Colonel's lady, a civil genteel woman. She had some resemblance of Tom Davies's 'mighty pretty wife'; at least she put me in mind of her. We found here too Donald Maclean, the young Laird of Coll (nephew to Talisker). I had a letter to him from his uncle, Professor MacLeod at Aberdeen. Mr Johnson said he was a fine fellow. He was a little brisk young man, had been a good deal in England studying farming, and was resolved to improve his father's lands without hurting the people or losing the ancient Highland fashions. He had seen Donald MacLeod at Loch Bracadale, who had been paying some small debts which he owed to some of the emigrants, but had £21 of our money remaining, and was trying to muster up what he had given away of it. This was so far good news.

As you read the extract you might need to look up some of the words which you are not familiar with in a dictionary.

A SPEAKING AND LISTENING   **READING**   WRITING

When you have read the extract, answer the following questions.

- Can you identify particular words that tell you this extract was written about a trip to Scotland? For example, the word 'MacLeod' in the third line is a Scottish surname. How many other examples can you find?

- This piece was obviously written in a different time from the Bill Bryson extract in the previous unit. Are there any words or sentences that tell you Boswell's piece was written a long time ago?

- The writing is detailed and very descriptive. Little or no time is spent describing the thoughts and feelings of either the people involved or the writer. Why do you think that this is the case?

You are now going to try and produce your own piece of detailed writing. Think about a place that you have visited, perhaps on holiday or on a visit to relatives who live a long way away from you. In no more than 300 words, write an account which describes in detail:

- what the town or city you visited was like
- the people that you met when you were there, e.g.
  - what they looked like
  - what you thought of them
- the place where you stayed
- the things that you did when you were there.

Remember that when trying to describe places, people and events in as much detail as possible, adjectives and adverbs are particularly useful words to use, so that the reader gets a full picture of your account.

Review

In this unit you have learned that:

- not all travel writing needs to be funny
- one of the main purposes of travel writing is to inform the reader and to describe in detail, the places, people and events which the writer comes across in her/his travels.

www.news.com

Aims

- To learn about how information is presented in an interactive medium – in this case, the World Wide Web, or as it is more commonly known, the Internet.

Starter session

Your teacher will write up on the board ten headlines which s/he has selected at random from the front and inside pages of a recent daily or Sunday newspaper. Your task is to place them in the order they interest you, with 1 being the most interesting and 10 being the one you find least interesting. For each headline, you should give a short explanation as to why you have given it that particular number.

- If a headline appeared like 'Anti-Pollution campaigners arrested for protest at chemical plant' and you placed it at No.1 in your rank order, the reason you might give for placing it first could be that you are very interested in the environment and the spread of pollution worldwide.

- If a headline appeared like 'Becks' foot has little chance of mending in time for World Cup clash' and you placed it at No.10 in your rank order, the reason you might give for placing it last could be that either you do not know who 'Becks' refers to (unlikely), or that you do not like David Beckham, or that you do not like football.

When you have ranked the headlines, your teacher will go around the class asking for your rank order and the reasons why you have placed them in that order. It should be possible to arrive at a final rank order which shows how interested you feel as a class about each of the original ten headlines.

Introduction

The Internet is a rapidly growing source of information and news. Many of you will already be experts at 'logging on' to the Internet and visiting your favourite websites. The amount of information which appears on the Internet is enormous. It is growing everyday, as new websites appear (and old ones disappear, for example through lack of 'traffic' – the number of visits or 'hits' to a particular site).

The Internet is an **interactive** means of communication. This means that the reader (or 'surfer') of the web does not simply soak up information which is presented to them passively, like a sponge. The reader actually has some control over how much information they wish to take in. This is where the notion of interactivity applies.

Development

A SPEAKING AND LISTENING   **READING**   WRITING

Look at the web pages which appear below. They are taken from the BBC's *Newsround* website. Many of you will be familiar with the BBC news programme for young people – *Newsround*. This is the website for that programme.

As you read, think about the following issues.

- There is a lot of information presented in these web pages. How easy do you find it to read the information? Comment on the design and layout of the pages.

- How would you know that this was a news website aimed at young people? Give some examples to support your answer.

- How much choice do you think you have over which particular bits of information you wish to read? Support your answer by reference to the web pages.

- What other ways are there of receiving the information other than by reading it? How do you know this?

- There are at least two other ways in which these pages might be described as interactive. Can you identify them?

You are now going to try and design your own 'home' page for your school's website. Remember that it should be designed for pupils of your own age. (It might be that your school already has its own website, but this is likely to have been designed with adults – parents who might want to get their children into your school – in mind.) Before you begin writing:

- remind yourself of the way that the information was presented in the extracts above
- think carefully about the sorts of information which would appeal to young people, e.g.

most popular/least popular subjects on the timetable

favourite/least favourite teachers   headteacher   sports facilities

school clubs   school swots   school bullies

- think about the ways to make your site interactive, e.g.
  – voting on the most popular school dinners.

These are just some of the areas which could be included, but you will be able to think of many more.

Review

In this unit you have learned about the way that information is presented on a website. You have also learned that:

- the Internet allows you some choice on which aspects of the information you wish to read, listen to or see
- interactivity allows you to feed back on the information which is presented, e.g. voting on issues or emailing the site, and so affect how the information is updated or presented in the future.

David and Ann prefer Mercury!

Aims

- To learn more about the language of persuasion as used in printed adverts.

Starter session

The list below identifies a range of different types of writing or texts. With a partner, try to decide whether each text is a fiction or non-fiction text. (Remember that a fiction text is one that is 'made up' by the writer; and that a non-fiction text is 'real').

- a cookbook recipe
- a play by Shakespeare
- an autobiography
- a newspaper article
- a video of a film
- a bus ticket
- a novel by Charles Dickens
- a biography of Charles Dickens
- a pop music magazine
- a short story by Roald Dahl
- a book on travel writing
- a book of children's nursery rhymes

Once you have identified these texts as either fiction or non-fiction, go on to try and say whether you think that they are literary or non-literary. Once you have finished, your teacher will ask for your answers, and will discuss with the whole of the class each of the texts listed.

Introduction

In general, we see **fiction** as being writing that is 'made up' or invented. Therefore, a story like Charles Dickens' *Oliver Twist* is fictional, as it was an invention of Dickens' imagination (even though he might have got the original idea from some real-life situation or people). On the other hand, we tend to see **non-fiction** as writing based on the truth and the facts. Therefore, a newspaper report on a train crash would be seen as non-fiction, as it is based on something that actually happened.

A problem arises, however, when we try to further classify texts as either **literary** or **non-literary**. Literary texts are normally seen as having a connection to the three main types of English literature:

- poems
- novels
- plays

And these three literary forms are traditionally seen as fictional.

However, many types of non-fiction may also be written in a literary style, for example:

- biographies
- autobiographies
- journals
- travel writing and so on

as this book attempts to show.

What is clear is that although we might be able to decide with some amount of certainty whether a text is either fiction or non-fiction, it is much more difficult to clearly identify whether it is a literary or non-literary text.

Development

Advertisers use persuasive language to try and get us to buy a range of goods and services. Unless they are using blatant lies to sell their products, this type of writing is normally classified as factual, and therefore non-fictional.

In recent years, however, in order to attract the interest of the public, many advertisers have used a literary style to advertise their products, by linking their adverts to a poem, a play or a novel. Shakespeare's plays, for example, are a favourite source of inspiration for advertisers.

There was a recent TV advert for Carling lager which was based on a scene from *Hamlet*, with Yorick's skull being used as a football, using the catchline 'on me head, son!'

Look at the advert which appears opposite.

Mummy is calling Grandpa.
She is using Mercury because it is a long distance call.

Does Grandpa need Mercury before mummy can call him? asks Ann.

No, says David. You can call any telephone anywhere with Mercury.

When I grow up, I want to work for Mercury, says Ann.

David, Ann and mummy like Mercury.

Daddy likes the car.

key words:
Mercury   call   any   telephone

FreeCall 0500 500 400 (residential) or FreeCall 0500 700 100 (business) any time

After you have read it, answer the following questions.

- What is the advert selling? Give examples from the writing to support your answer.
- Does the picture give any clues as to what is being advertised?
- Does the advert remind you of any books which you have come across? Think about your earlier school years! Give examples from the extract.

The advert above is a piece of non-fiction, based on the facts about Mercury communications, but which actually uses a literary style (normally associated with fiction) to get its message across. It is clearly written in the style of the 'Janet and John' type of reading books that you might have come across in primary school. These early reading books had the following features:

- they were clearly fictional
- they were written using mainly simple sentences

- they normally contained the following characters:
  - a daddy
  - a mummy
  - a boy
  - a girl.
- colourful pictures were used to support a simple story.

This advert is a good example of the lack of any clear divide between fiction, non-fiction, literary and non-literary texts.

B SPEAKING AND LISTENING   READING   **WRITING**

You are going to try and produce your own advert, written in a literary style. Your task is to write a poem in no more than 14 lines, but no less than 5 lines, to advertise one of the products or services listed below. It will probably help you if you give your product or service an actual name, e.g. a treatment cream for acne or spots might be called something like 'Zitto'.

> a mobile phone   a beauty parlour
>
> a treatment cream for acne or spots   a computer supplier
>
> a model of car   soap powder   a slimming diet
>
> a breakfast cereal   a computer game   a pair of trainers

Review

In this unit you have learned that it is sometimes difficult to classify texts as being:
- either fictional
- or non-fictional
- and/or literary
- and/or non-literary.

In many instances, the boundaries between these ways of classifying texts are blurred. In reality, texts can have some of the features of all four types of text. This is increasingly the case with adverts, as advertisers try to find new ways of persuading us to buy their goods and services.

Save the planet

Aims

- To learn that some types of writing which appear to be fictional, and therefore made up or invented by the writer, actually carry a very serious message.

Starter session

Most of the nursery rhymes or stories that you came across as a child actually contain a serious message or moral. For example, here is a quick summary of the story 'The hare and the tortoise'. A hare and a tortoise agree to race against each other. Due to his speed, the hare should win easily; but because he is overconfident, he takes a nap half-way through the race. The tortoise overtakes him as he is sleeping and actually wins the race.

The moral of the story is something along the lines that 'if you take things steady, you are more likely to win, than if you sprint off at the start'.

Think of another children's story. When you have chosen one, raise your hand and tell it to the rest of the class, ending with what you think the moral or message behind the story is.

Introduction

'The hare and the tortoise' is one story in a famous collection of tales known as *Aesop's Fables*. Aesop was a Greek slave who lived from 620BC to 560BC.

A **fable** is a story which is intended to teach a moral lesson. Using the technique of re-telling a non-fictional story through a fable, can sometimes be a good way of discussing whether people's behaviour is correct and proper. Fables are, therefore, an interesting way of looking at real, non-fictional issues and events.

Development

Look at the extract which appears below. It is written by Rachel Carson, who is well-known for her writing on pollution and environmental issues.

A Fable for Tomorrow

para 1 THERE WAS ONCE a town in the heart of America where all life seemed to live in harmony with its surroundings. The town lay in the midst of a checkerboard of prosperous farms, with fields of grain and hillsides of orchards where, in spring, white clouds of bloom drifted above the green fields. In autumn, oak and maple and birch set up a blaze of colour that flamed and flickered across a backdrop of pines. Then foxes barked in the hills and deer silently crossed the fields, half hidden in the mists of the autumn mornings.

para 2 Along the roads, laurel, viburnum and alder, great ferns and wildflowers delighted the traveller's eye through much of the year. Even in winter the roadsides were places of beauty, where countless birds came to feed on the berries and on the seed heads of the dried weeds rising above the snow. The countryside was, in fact, famous for the abundance and variety of its bird life, and when the flood of migrants was pouring through in spring and autumn people travelled from great distances to observe them. Others came to fish the streams, which flowed clear and cold out of the hills and contained shady pools where trout lay. So it had been from the days many years ago when the first settlers raised their houses, sank their wells, and built their barns.

para 3 Then a strange blight crept over the area and everything began to change. Some evil spell had settled on the community: mysterious maladies swept the flocks of chickens; the cattle and sheep sickened and died. Everywhere was a shadow of death. The farmers spoke of much illness among their families. In the town the doctors had become more and more puzzled by new kinds of sickness appearing among their patients. There had been several sudden and unexplained deaths, not only among adults but even among children, who would be stricken suddenly while at play and die within a few hours.

para 4 There was a strange stillness. The birds, for example – where had they gone? Many people spoke of them, puzzled and disturbed. The feeding stations in the backyards were deserted. The few birds seen anywhere were moribund; they trembled violently and could not fly. It was a spring without voices. On the mornings that had once throbbed with the dawn chorus of robins, catbirds, doves, jays, wrens, and scores of other bird voices there was now no sound; only silence lay over the fields and woods and marsh.

para 5 On the farms the hens brooded, but no chicks hatched. The farmers complained that they were unable to raise any pigs – the litters were small and the young survived only a few days. The apple trees were coming into bloom but no bees droned among the blossoms, so there was no pollination and there would be no fruit.

para 6 The roadsides, once so attractive, were now lined with browned and withered vegetation as though swept by fire. These, too, were silent, deserted by all living things. Even the streams were now lifeless. Anglers no longer visited them, for all the fish had died.

para 7 In the gutters under the eaves and between the shingles of the roofs, a white granular powder still showed a few patches; some weeks before it had fallen like snow upon the roofs and the lawns, the fields and streams.

para 8 No witchcraft, no enemy action had silenced the rebirth of new life in this stricken world. The people had done it themselves.

para 9 This town does not actually exist, but it might easily have a thousand counterparts in America or elsewhere in the world. I know of no community that has experienced all the misfortunes I describe. Yet every one of these disasters has actually happened somewhere, and many real communities have already suffered a substantial number of them. A grim spectre has crept upon us almost unnoticed, and this imagined tragedy may easily become a stark reality we all shall know.

Vocabulary

viburnum – a shrub with white flowers

moribund – at the point of death

A SPEAKING AND LISTENING   **READING**   WRITING

As you read, try to answer the following questions.

- Apart from the obvious clue of the title of the extract, can you identify anything in the style of the writing which might suggest connections to stories for children?

- In the first two paragraphs, what kind of picture is the author trying to create?

- Thinking along the same lines, what is happening in paragraphs 3, 4, 5, 6 and 7?

- What effect is being created in paragraph 8?

- What is the point of paragraph 9?

- Do you think that the writer gets her message across in a strong and effective way?

Give reasons for your answers.

You are now going to try and produce your own fable in order to draw a moral lesson relating to a real-life, non-fictional issue. Choose one of the issues listed below:

- the case against the chemical pollution of the oceans
- the case against nuclear power
- the case for cancer research testing on animals
- the case against the return of capital punishment
- the case for compulsory wearing of school uniform
- the case against smoking tobacco.

Your task is to create a fictional story in no more than 300 words, based on your chosen issue in order to make a serious, real-life point.

- If you chose the case against capital punishment, your story might be built around the following main points:
  - a person is wrongly arrested and convicted for murder
  - s/he is sentenced to death in the electric chair
  - after the execution, evidence comes to light to prove her/his innocence.

The moral of this story would be that capital punishment is wrong because you can never be 100 per cent sure that the law has tried and convicted the person responsible for a crime.

Review

In this unit you have learned that one of the ways that we can address real-life, non-fictional issues is by writing about it in the style of a fable. The main features of fable are that they

- contain a moral message
- are fictional, but through careful choice of characters, setting and plot, can focus on a serious issue or event
- are another example of the blurring of the boundaries between fiction and non-fiction.

An event that shook the world

Aims

- To learn about public speaking; in particular, the techniques used by politicians to hold the interest of their listeners or readers.

Starter session

With a partner, look at the lists below and try to match each famous person to the famous phrase with which they are associated.

List A	List B
1. 'Friends, Romans, countrymen, lend me your ears...'	1. Sherlock Holmes
2. 'I have a dream...'	2. Mark Twain (American humorist and writer)
3. 'Never, in the field of human conflict, has so much *been* owed by so many to so few...'	3. Macbeth (in the play of the same name by Shakespeare)
4. 'I can never tell a lie...'	4. Mohammed Ali (former heavyweight boxing champion of the world)
5. 'Reports of my death have been greatly exaggerated...'	5. George Washington (1st president of theUnited States of America)
6. 'Is this a dagger I *see* before me?'	6. Admiral Lord Nelson (just before his death at the battle of Trafalgar)
7. 'One small step for man, one giant leap for mankind'	7. Winston Churchill (Prime Minister of Britain during World War II)
8. 'I am The Greatest'	8. Neil Armstrong (first man to set foot on the moon)
9. 'Elementary, my dear Watson'	9. Mark Antony (in Shakespeare's Julius Ceasar)
10. 'Kiss me, Hardy'	10. Dr Martin Luther King (American Civil Rights campaigner in the 1960s)

When you have finished raise your hand and read one of your 'matches' out to the rest of the class. Your teacher will tell you if you are right or wrong.

Introduction

You may have come across the word 'rhetoric' in your English studies. A rhetorical question is one which is asked but does not expect a reply. The question is asked in order to make a statement, rather than to get an answer. For example, if a footballer deliberately commits a foul and is penalised by the referee, he might react by asking 'What have I done ref?' usually throwing his arms up in the air in disbelief! The footballer obviously knows what he has done – committed a foul – but asks the question and makes the gesture with his arms, in order to falsely protest his innocence.

More generally, rhetoric means the manipulation of language in order to persuade or influence an audience. There are even rhetorical techniques, or 'devices', which have been used for hundreds of years. This kind of rhetoric is often used in public speaking and it involves using language which appears to be important and clever, grand and impressive, often spoken in a forceful and dramatic way.

Rhetoric tends to be used by politicians – who do a lot of public speaking – in order to try and persuade us to their point of view. Political rhetoric can be very effective, and many politicians employ professional speech writers who are very skilled in the art of rhetoric. One rhetorical device, often used in writing speeches, involves putting ideas, statements or points in an argument into groups of three, with the emphasis being put on the third part. The famous quote from Shakespeare's *Julius Caesar*, 'Friends, Romans, countrymen...' is an example of this device in action.

Development

Look at the extract which appears opposite. It is taken from a speech made by George W Bush, the current President of the United States, on the evening of 11 September 2001, the day that the terrorist suicide plane attacks took place on the twin towers of the World Trade Centre in New York and The Pentagon in Washington.

This extract from the President's speech is a particularly good example of the use of rhetoric to try and persuade the American people to view the terrorist attacks in a particular way.

Good evening. Today, our fellow citizens, our way of life, our very freedom came under attack in a series of deliberate and deadly terrorist acts. The victims were in airplanes, or in their offices; secretaries, businessmen and women, military and federal workers; moms and dads, friends and neighbors. Thousands of lives were suddenly ended by evil, despicable acts of terror.

The pictures of airplanes flying into buildings, fires burning, huge structures collapsing, have filled us with disbelief, terrible sadness, and a quiet, unyielding anger. These acts of mass murder were intended to frighten our nation into chaos and retreat. But they have failed; our country is strong.

A great people has been moved to defend a great nation. Terrorist attacks can shake the foundations of our biggest buildings, but they cannot touch the foundation of America. These acts shattered steel, but they cannot dent the steel of American resolve.

America was targeted for attack because we're the brightest beacon for freedom and opportunity in the world. And no one will keep that light from shining.

Today, our nation saw evil, the very worst of human nature. And we responded with the best of America – with the daring of our rescue workers, with the caring for strangers and neighbours who came to give blood and help in any way they could.

A SPEAKING AND LISTENING **READING** WRITING

After you have read the extract (you may need to read it more than once to get its full meaning) consider the following issues:

- How many examples of rhetorical language can you identify?

- Try to explain why you think it is rhetorical.

- See if you can identify any examples of the trick of grouping words, phrases, statements or points of an argument, into groups of three for effect.

- If possible, present your findings in a table as shown below, using ICT.

Example of rhetoric	Reason why it is rhetorical	Groups of three
'...our very freedom came under attack...'	it is an exaggeration – Americans are still very free following the attacks	'...our fellow citizens, our way of life, our very freedom...'

You are now going to produce your own piece of rhetorical writing.

Imagine that your school has a School Council which is made up of both teachers and students. The job of the School Council is to have responsibility for a range of non-teaching matters within the school, for example:

- the quality of the school lunches and the different dishes on the menu
- the running of the school tuck shop
- the running of the school radio station which broadcasts for 1 hour at lunchtimes
- the running of the various school clubs
- the running of the school theatre
- access to the on-site sports centre.

Your task is to write a political speech – in no more than 300 words – setting out why students and staff should vote for you to get elected onto the Council.

- Before you write, remind yourself of the style of writing used in the political speech above, and try to use a similar style for your speech.
- Include points on the following:
  - the weaknesses of the current School Council, e.g. that it might not be very effective at influencing matters which come within its responsibility
  - the weaknesses of some of the current student representatives on the Council
  - how you would propose to change matters so that more relevant issues might be discussed by the Council.

Review

In this unit you have investigated and analysed the use made of rhetorical devices in the style of writing that is common in public speaking and political speeches.

'What the Dickens!'

Aims

- To learn more about biographical writing – the story or aspects of someone's life, written by someone else.

Starter session

Think of someone well-known that you admire or who interests you – it could be a pop star, a football player, an actor or actress, or even a member of your family. List 10 facts which you know about the person that you have chosen which you think helps to describe the important parts of her/his life. For example, if you chose Mohammed Ali, who is known all over the world, you might list the following facts:

- born in Louisville, Kentucky, USA
- a very skilful boxer and former heavyweight champion of the world
- was regarded as boastful and big-headed
- a black man
- a muslim
- made lots of money from boxing
- refused to fight for America in the war in Vietnam in the late 1960s
- is world famous for things other than boxing
- has worked as a United Nations ambassador doing charity work in the developing world
- has met and made friends with most of the world politicians and heads of state.

When you have finished listing your ten points, raise your hand and tell them to the rest of the class.

Introduction

In order to be effective, good biographical writing needs to contain enough detail concerning the person being written about, to:

- keep the interest of the reader
- convince them that the writer is giving an accurate picture of that person's life.

Of course, the facts about someone's life may be interpreted in different ways by different biographers. For example:

- There are many biographies which have been written about the life of the late Princess of Wales, Princess Diana.
- Some writers are very sympathetic to her concerning her relationship with the press, seeing her as being hounded and pursued unfairly by the press ever since she became engaged to marry Prince Charles.
- Other writers see her as being highly skilled at using the press to promote her own image in a positive way.
- The facts about the late Princess's relationship with the press exist, but obviously, they can be interpreted in different ways depending on the point of view of the biographer.

Development

Look at the extract which appears opposite. It is taken from a well-known biography of the writer Charles Dickens, written by Peter Ackroyd, a famous modern biographer. Dickens's novels, as you might be aware, were set in nineteenth-century Victorian England, and drew attention to the harsh and often cruel social conditions of the times.

Amongst Dickens's most famous novels are *A Christmas Carol*, *David Copperfield*, *Great Expectations*, *Hard Times*, *Nicholas Nickleby* and *Pickwick Papers*. This extract from Ackroyd's biography is about the origins of what is probably Dickens's most famous novel, *Oliver Twist*.

Dickens

The first number of the new magazine, in January 1837, had opened with a sketch by him [Dickens] entitled 'The Public Life of Mr Tulrumble' and then the next month another sketch, a continuation of the first, appeared under the title 'Oliver Twist'. The first had been set in 'Mudfog' a pseudonym for Chatham, and was a pleasant enough satire on the idiocies of provincial authorities with the moral that 'puffed-up conceit is not dignity'. The second, with 'Oliver Twist' as its title, begins in a workhouse in the same town of Mudfog. In other words, at this point, harassed by family difficulties, exhausted by overwork, and suffering from a variety of ailments, Dickens himself did not at first seem to realise that he was embarking upon the novel which in later years would perhaps more than any other be identified with his name. He had the idea only of a series of articles in mind ('The Chronicles of Mudfog' perhaps), but then almost as soon as he began he found that he had 'hit on a capital notion'. For he had created the figure of Oliver, the child born and brought up in a workhouse, the child who dared to ask for more, and at once he saw the possibilities which could be extracted from it. The idea of a series of sketches was abandoned.

What is clear is that as soon as Dickens had hit upon his 'capital notion' of the deprived and abused child, the whole conception caught fire in his imagination. It is even possible that this was in essence the 'proposed Novel' which he had been contemplating ever since he began seriously to write, and it has been said, rightly, that Oliver Twist is the first novel in the English language which takes a child as its central character or hero; a revolution, perhaps, although not one which was widely noticed at the time. This is largely because factual 'orphan tales' were actually quite common in the period, and Dickens himself had often read autobiographies which emphasise the miseries and privations of childhood: even Johnson's life of Richard Savage has a long passage on the horrors of his infancy. There was also an ancient but still healthy tradition of 'rogue literature' which in part chronicled the dramas of lost or abandoned children. So the theme of Oliver Twist was not in that respect new. Nevertheless it was one that directly appealed to Dickens's own sense of himself and his past, and was therefore one in which all the resources of his imagination could be poured. In the original sketch Oliver was born in Mudfog or Chatham, the site of Dickens's own infancy, and the figure of the parish boy's 'progress' was one that at once attracted a cluster of childhood feelings and associations. Oliver Twist's forced association with Fagin, which seems like a savage reprise of the young Dickens's companionship with Bob Fagin in the blacking factory; Oliver's flight towards respectability; his journey from dirt to cleanliness and gentility. Thus does Dickens seem able to work through his own childhood in disguised form, both in its troubled reality and in its disturbed fantasies of escape.

After you have read the extract, consider the following:

● Do you think that Ackroyd adopts a sympathetic or antagonistic approach to Dickens? Support your answer with examples from the extract.

● Can you identify an example from the extract where Ackroyd appears to be interpreting the facts in a particular way?

● Give five examples from the extract of details which Ackroyd must have researched in detail before being able to include it in his biography of Dickens.

You are now going to produce a piece of biographical writing of your own. Think back to the starter activity and the well-known personality that you chose the ten facts about. Or, if you like, choose someone else as the subject for your short biography. Based on the facts which you have listed, write your interpretation of them in order to provide a short, but fairly detailed biographical account of your subject. You should use no more than 250 words.

Review

In this unit you have learned some more about the technique of biographical writing, and in particular, that:

● before you write, there is a need to establish the facts about your subject's life

● this might involve some detailed research

● these facts will be interpreted by you in a particular way

● both sympathetic and less sympathetic interpretations can emerge from the same set of facts depending on the point of view of the writer

● the more details which are gathered, the more likely the biography is to be truthful.

Save it!

Aims

- To learn about writing which advises, offers alternatives, and takes into account the possible consequences of taking or not taking the particular advice offered.

Starter session

In your school there will be someone who is responsible for Careers' Advice – a teacher or other adult whose job it is to advise pupils on the sorts of careers which they might like to take up when they leave school. Working with a partner:

- Choose a job or career that you think you might like to follow when you leave school.
- If you are unsure what you want to do when you leave school, choose an imaginary job or career.
- List six points which you think are important skills necessary for the career or job you have chosen.
- When you have finished, swap lists with your partner and discuss.
- Are there any points which your partner has listed which you haven't?
- Produce a final list of aspects about the career or job.
- Raise your hand and read your list out to the rest of the class.

Introduction

Unless you are extremely confident and very bright, you will probably feel the need to take some advice before starting to do something new.

This is certainly the case for most big decisions which you are faced with. But it also relates to many other less important areas of life. Think about the factors you might be likely to consider before buying a new car. The main ones would be:

- price
- safety
- comfort
- speed

- road handling
- fuel economy
- looks/colour
- luggage space

- air conditioning
- electric windows
- stereo system.

It might be that if you chose a new car mainly because of its speed (e.g. a sports car) you might have to 'trade off' some element of safety and comfort. In this case, it is important that the advice you are given is as full as possible, and allows you to make an informed decision. It is also important that you are aware of the consequences of that decision.

Development

Look at the advice leaflet which appears here. It is produced by a national bank – The Halifax – in order to advise young people how to manage their money, and in particular, the advantages in saving it.

How save4it works

When you open your account you'll get a passbook. You'll need this to pay money in or take money out at any Halifax branch. When you pay money in, you'll get a save4it receipt. You can put this on your wall and see how much cash you've got.

How to get your save4it account

It's really easy...

Just speak to your parents or another adult in your family. You'll need to bring in some identification, like your birth certificate or passport. Next time you're in a Halifax branch, ask a member of staff if you can open a save4it account. You can open a save4it account if you are aged between 7 and 16 years old. If you're under 7, the account will have to be opened by an adult for you.

So what are you waiting for?

the account that's your very own

get your hands on one today --------->

Want one?

save4it is the new account that helps you save for the things you want to buy. Start saving now and watch your money grow. Whatever you're saving for, you could soon have enough money to splash out on that new football shirt, the latest CD or a computer game.

HALIFAX **save 4 it**

my savings account

What else? Cool!

✓ Your very own passbook
✓ An account that you can name
✓ Interest added to your account once a year on any date you choose, like Christmas or your birthday.

Q. What is interest?

A. Interest is the money your account earns over a year. For example if you had £100 in your account all year and the interest rate stayed at 5%, you would get £5 interest on your savings on your chosen interest date. Of course the interest rate and the amount you've saved could change over the year, but the money in your account will always be earning interest, helping you save up for the things you want.

can't wait to get your stuff? --------->

A

After you have read the leaflet, consider the following:

- How would you know that this leaflet is aimed specifically at young people rather than adults?
- Is there anything particularly noteworthy about the title of the leaflet and the way in which it is written?
- List three advantages of opening a 'save 4 it' account
- Why do you think banks produce leaflets like this to try and get young people to save? Would you be persuaded to save after having read this leaflet?
- Who do you think would benefit more from following the advice contained in the leaflet – young people or the bank? Give reasons for your answer.

You are now going to produce your own advice leaflet.

These days there is a lot of pressure on young people to stay on at school or college after the age of 16, and continue with their education. It is likely that you, too, will have to face this issue in a couple of years' time when you have finished sitting your GCSE examinations at the end of Year 11.

Your task is to write an advice sheet for Year 11 students advising them of the advantages of continuing their education rather than leaving to find a job. The following is a list of the sorts of factors which you might need to consider before making a decision:

- the need to get good GCSE grades and A-level qualifications for work purposes
- whether you would wish some day to go on to university
- the general benefits of being well-educated, that might not be directly related to getting a job, for example your own personal development.

Also, try to set out clearly, the consequences of not continuing your education, raising issues like

- unemployment   ● poorly skilled jobs   ● low pay
- low opinion of yourself.

Remember that to be successful, the advice leaflet has to appeal to young people like yourself. If it is possible, use ICT to add some visual images to your leaflet thus adding, hopefully, to its impact.

Review

In this unit you have learned that writing which persuades, argues and advises.

- needs to be detailed and offer clear alternatives so that informed choices can be made by those who it is intended to advise
- needs to be clear about the consequences of either following or not following the advice offered
- needs to be relevant to its target audience and presented in an attractive way.

Our school's the business!

Aims

- To learn more about *why* it is important to provide clear and precise information, written and presented with an appropriate degree of formality.

Starter session

Choose a subject that interests you and that you know a fair amount of detail about. For example, it might be a sporting activity:

- football
- cricket
- table tennis
- badminton
- tennis

or a different kind of hobby or interest:

- train spotting
- music
- drama
- reading
- painting

Choose an interest which appeals to you and quickly prepare a formal spoken presentation to the class explaining what you think are its attractions. Your presentation should:

- be written and presented in Standard English
- take no more than one minute in length.

When you have finished preparing, raise your hand and read your presentation out to the rest of the class. As a class, you should vote on the speech that contained the most information and was presented most effectively.

Introduction

We all tend to have something that holds our interest. It might be a hobby or a sporting activity. But equally, it could be something a bit more serious, like helping old people or another sort of voluntary work. Knowing about something that interests you, however, and being able to explain it to an audience are two very different things. As you progress through school and life in general, you will be asked to explain *why*.

For example, in English, you will increasingly be asked to give your opinions on why you preferred one book to another. Being able to give your own opinion on such matters will certainly get you better marks in your English examinations! Being able to express your views clearly and formally, using Standard English, is a very important skill which you will need to master. You will have to give clear *reasons* for the choices you make over a wide range of issues.

Development

Look at the extract which appears below.

curriculum

Our fundamental aim is to provide challenging learning experiences that enable our students to achieve their potential. The curriculum is broad, balanced, challenging and relevant.

The standard length of lesson is 50 minutes. We believe that this is the optimum length for concise delivery while simultaneously offering sufficient opportunities for development and extension work.

Excluding breaks, registration, assemblies and form periods students are taught for 25 hours per week.

Key Stage 3

Students are taught in form groups for year 7. From year 8 onwards, they are placed in differentiated teaching groups in English, Mathematics, Science and Modern Languages. Most students are placed in 'Challenge sets', where they are enabled to realise their capabilities. Those students who show good aptitude in a subject follow an 'Accelerated' programme where they aim for the very highest examination grades. In some subjects, where staffing permits, students who require more individual teacher attention are placed in smaller 'Support' groups. All students take the following courses: English Language and Literature, Mathematics, Science, Modern Foreign Languages, History, Geography, Art, Technology, Physical Education, Music, Religious Education, Personal and Social Education including Study Skills, Information and Communication Technology.

Key Stage 4

Our policy is to incorporate the maximum amount of choice available from our resources. We currently offer three option lines of full GCSE course. The option lines for courses beginning in September 2002 are printed in an insert. All students experience the world of work at this stage of their career at Stretford when they take part in a one week placement.

Sixth Form

Each year large numbers of students join the sixth form from other institutions. As a Grammar School, the academic qualifications that we offer are A levels, which consist of two stages; AS and A2. AS is a lower level examination that students complete in the first year before beginning an A2 course. The current option lines are printed on an insert. All students study four subjects for AS in the Lower Sixth. Many then choose to continue with only three, when they study General Studies, or they continue with all four.

The Sixth form curriculum includes the Wednesday afternoon programme of either Games, Community Service or Work Experience. Time is also devoted to preparing for Higher Education, including visits to Careers Fairs and an Industry Conference.

This text is taken from the school prospectus of a well-known secondary school in the Manchester area, but it is likely that your school will also have its own prospectus. A prospectus is a document which gives lots of information about a school or college mainly to try and persuade parents to send their children there.

After you have read the extract consider the following.

- How easy do you find it to follow the information contained in the leaflet? Give an example.

- Can you identify any examples of *explanation* in the leaflet?

- The extract is written in a formal style – in written Standard English. Why do you think this is the case? Would a colloquial or slang style of writing have been better? Give reasons for your answer.

B   SPEAKING AND LISTENING   READING   **WRITING**

You are now going to try and produce your own piece of informative writing in Standard English.

As part of their prospectuses, most schools or colleges would include information on a range of school policies, not directly related to teaching. One of these is likely to concern the school's views on the matter of discipline.

Your task is to write the entry in the school prospectus on school discipline. Remember that your piece has to be written in a formal style and be able to explain clearly why discipline is important to the successful running of the school. You should concentrate on the following:

- why discipline is necessary
- the advantages of a good record on discipline – for both individual students and the school as a whole
- how discipline is recorded and who records it
- how individual student's discipline is communicated to parents
- what areas of school activity are covered by discipline
- what sorts of punishments are applied for poor discipline
- how those guilty of misbehaviour are helped to improve.

Review

In this unit you have looked at how clear explanations need to be given on a wide range of issues, events and situations. Increasingly, you will come under pressure to explain formally – and usually in writing – the reasons why you have made one particular choice rather than another.